APPOINTED
TO
LEADERSHIP

God's Principles
for
Spiritual Leaders

Jack W. Hayford
with
Herman Rosenberger

THOMAS NELSON PUBLISHERS
Nashville • Atlanta • London • Vancouver

DEDICATION

This, the third series of *Spirit-Filled Life
Bible Study Guides,* is dedicated to the
memory of

Dr. Roy H. Hicks, Jr.
(1944–1994)

one of God's "men for all seasons,"
faithful in the Word, mighty in the Spirit,
leading multitudes into the love of God
and the worship of His Son, Jesus Christ.

Unto Christ's glory and in Roy's memory,
we will continue to sing:

Praise the Name of Jesus,
Praise the Name of Jesus,
He's my Rock, He's my Fortress,
He's my Deliverer, in Him will I trust.
Praise the Name of Jesus.

Appointed to Leadership:
God's Principles for Spiritual Leaders
Copyright © 1994 by Jack W. Hayford

Published in Nashville, Tennessee, by Thomas Nelson, Inc.

Printed in the United States of America
9 10 11 12 13 14 15 16 - 02 01 00 99 98 97

CONTENTS

· ·

Appointed to Leadership: God's Principles for Spiritual Leaders is one of a series of study guides that focus exciting, discovery-geared coverage of Bible book and power themes—all prompting dynamic, Holy Spirit-filled living.

About the Executive Editor

JACK W. HAYFORD, noted pastor, teacher, writer, and composer, is the Executive Editor of the complete series, working with the publisher in the conceiving and developing of each of the books.

Dr. Hayford is Senior Pastor of The Church On The Way, the First Foursquare Church of Van Nuys, California. He and his wife, Anna, have four married children, all of whom are active in either pastoral ministry or vital church life. As General Editor of the *Spirit-Filled Life Bible*, Pastor Hayford led a four-year project, which has resulted in the availability of one of today's most practical and popular study Bibles. He is author of more than twenty books, including *A Passion for Fullness, The Beauty of Spiritual Language, Rebuilding the Real You*, and *Prayer Is Invading the Impossible*. His musical compositions number over four hundred songs, including the widely sung "Majesty."

About the Writer

HERMAN ROSENBERGER, with over forty years in public ministry, serves as Staff Pastor of the Ventura, California, Foursquare Church. He is actively involved in a writing ministry, having worked with both Gospel Light Publications and David C. Cook Publishers. His fruitful ministry in pastoral ministry served congregations in Monmouth, Illinois; Chicago Heights, Illinois; Rhinelander, Wisconsin; and Granada Hills, California. He also served as a professor and as Dean of Students at his alma mater from 1969–1976.

He earned his Bachelor of Theology degree from LIFE Bible College in Los Angeles, following his service in the Navy after World War II. He has the Bachelor's and the Master's degrees from Azusa Pacific (University) and attended Moody Bible Institute.

Herman is married to Margaret (Gomez) and has four children: Judith (deceased), Sharon, Katherine, and Deborah. Sharon and Katherine are engaged in Christian leadership; Deborah and her husband, Fouch Dayton Fuller, pastor a congregation in Vallejo, California.

Of this contributor, the Executive Editor has remarked: "There are few men I've met who combine the admirable qualities of gracious gentlemanliness and a meticulous attention to detail as does Herman. He is a man of precision in scholarship, conversation, public discourse, and personal duty—yet while so demanding of himself, he keeps a breadth of openness toward the many of us so very much less capable of his blend of perfect courtesy. He's a Holy-Spirit-filled model of Christian generosity."

THE KEYS
THAT KEEP ON FREEING

And I will give you the keys of the kingdom of heaven, and whatever you bind on earth will be bound in heaven, and whatever you loose on earth will be loosed in heaven. (Matt. 16:19)

While there is no conclusive list of exactly what keys Jesus was referring to, it is clear that He did confer upon His church—upon *all* who believe—the access to a realm of spiritual partnership with Him in the dominion of His kingdom. The "keys" to this partnership are *concepts*—biblical themes that promote spiritual vitality when applied with faith under the lordship of Jesus Christ. The "partnership" is the *essential* feature of this release of divine grace; (1) believers reach to *receive* Christ's promise of "kingdom keys," (2) while choosing to *believe* in the Holy Spirit's readiness to unleash their power today.

Companions to the Bible book studies in the *Spirit-Filled Life Study Guide* series, the Kingdom Dynamic studies present a variety of different themes. This series is an outgrowth of the Kingdom Dynamics themes included throughout the *Spirit-Filled Life Bible*.

The central goal of this series of study guides is to help you discover "power points" of the Holy Spirit-filled life. Assisting you in your discoveries are a number of helpful features. Each study guide has twelve to fourteen lessons, each arranged so you can plumb the depths or skim the surface, depending upon your needs and interests. The study guides contain major lesson features, each marked by a symbol and heading for easy identification.

WORD WEALTH

The WORD WEALTH feature provides important definitions of key terms.

 ### BEHIND THE SCENES

BEHIND THE SCENES supplies information about cultural beliefs and practices, doctrinal disputes, business trades, and the like, that illuminate Bible passages and teachings.

 ### AT A GLANCE

The AT A GLANCE feature uses maps and charts to identify places and simplify themes or positions.

 ### KINGDOM EXTRA

Because this study guide focuses on a theme of the Bible, you will find a KINGDOM EXTRA feature that guides you into Bible dictionaries, Bible encyclopedias, and other resources that will enable you to glean more from the Bible's wealth on the topic if you want something extra.

 ### PROBING THE DEPTHS

Another feature, PROBING THE DEPTHS, will explain controversial issues raised by particular lessons and cite Bible passages and other sources to which you can turn to help you come to your own conclusions.

 ### FAITH ALIVE

Finally, lessons contain FAITH ALIVE feature. Here the focus is, So what? Given what the Bible says, what does it mean for my life? How can it impact my day-to-day needs, hurts, relationships, concerns, and whatever else is important to me? FAITH ALIVE will help you see and apply the practical relevance of God's literary gift.

As you'll see, these guides supply space for you to answer the study and life-application questions and exercises. You may, however, want to record all your answers, or just the overflow from your study or application, in a separate notebook or journal.

The Bible study method used in this series follows four basic steps. **Observation** answers the question, What does the text say? **Interpretation** deals with, What does the text mean? —not to you or me, but what it meant to its original readers. **Correlation** asks, What light do other Scripture passages shed on this text? And **application,** the goal of Bible study, poses the question, How should my life change in response to the Holy Spirit's teaching of this text?

If you have used a Bible much before, you know that it comes in a variety of translations and paraphrases. Although you can use any of them with profit as you work through the *Spirit-Filled Life Kingdom Dynamics Study Guide* series, when Bible passages or words are cited, you will find they are from the *New King James Version* of the Bible. Using this translation with this series will make your study easier, but it's certainly not necessary.

A word of warning, though. By itself, Bible study will not transform your life. Through Bible study, you will grow in your understanding of the Lord, His kingdom and your place in it, and those things are essential. But you need more. You need to rely on the Holy Spirit to guide your study and your application of the Bible's truths. He, Jesus promised, was sent to teach us "all things" (John 14:26; cf. 1 Cor. 2:13). So as you use this series to guide you through Scripture, bathe your study time in prayer, asking the Spirit of God to illuminate the text, enlighten your mind, humble your will, and comfort your heart. He will never let you down. He promises you!

Preface

If you are a person who wants to serve God's people and Jesus' Church in a spiritual leadership you will find *Appointed to Leadership* helpful in several ways.

This study guide will assist you in developing a sensitivity to the lessons and the promptings of the Holy Spirit in your life as He guides you into fruitful leadership ministry. It will

- Help you to respond with obedience to God's call on your life and to understand His purpose in the call more clearly.
- Enhance your understanding of the value of a godly lifestyle and the necessity of being totally committed as you serve in leadership.
- Show the way to confidence in ministry that flows out of a good relationship with God and will help you understand your spiritual gifting and personal identity.
- Suggest ways in which you may encourage faith in the hearts of the people whom you lead.
- Make clear what it means to lead God's people in the manner in which He would have them to be led, how to rely on the anointing of the Spirit, and why being open and approachable by others is crucial.
- Encourage you to believe for miracles, signs, and wonders to be manifested among the people whom you serve in leadership.

As you pursue this study, not only will you be humbled, challenged, and inspired; you will also become grateful to God for the opportunity to serve in His kingdom.

Lesson 1/Obedience to the Call

THE CALL

The biblical idea of God's calling is not simply that He invites men to serve Him. The call of God is more than that. You might say the calling of God is an invitation with clout in it. It is more like a summons. The summons comes through His Word and the power of the Holy Spirit laying hold of the one summoned, convincing him or her that God has spoken. The purpose of the call is that the one summoned might participate in and enjoy the blessed benefits of God's redemptive purposes and participate in the Great Commission to reach the world for Christ.

 WORD WEALTH

Call, *kaleo,* means: to call, or call to (John 10:3); to call into one's presence, send for a person (Matt. 2:7); to summon (Matt. 2:15, Matt. 25:14); to invite (Matt. 22:9); to call to the performance of a certain thing (Matt. 9:13; Heb. 11:8); to call to a participation in the privileges of the gospel (Rom. 8:30, 9:24; 1 Cor. 1:9, 7:18); to call to an office of dignity (Heb. 5:4).[1]

In the New Testament the idea of calling has to do with God's approach to the individual. In Matthew, Mark, Luke, and Acts, the term "call" denotes God's summons spoken by Christ or in His name.

Read the following verses and note the nature of the call, who is calling, and who is being called.

Mark 1:20

Mark 2:17; Luke 5:32

Acts 2:39

The following verses are about the call of God upon individuals. They reveal the particular functions and offices to which those individuals are assigned. Read the verses and identify the particular function or office to which the individual(s) is assigned.

Acts 13:2; 16:9, 10

Romans 1:1

Hebrews 5:4

CALLED, NOT DRIVEN

In his book *Transforming Leadership*, Leighton Ford writes, "Genuine leaders operate out of a sense of calling, not a sense of drivenness."[2] He adds, "The writer George MacDonald has said somewhere that real Christian leaders are people who are moved at God's pace and in God's time to God's place, not because they fancy themselves there, but because they are drawn."[3]

The call of God to a place of leadership may come in a variety of ways:

- When alone with God in a time of prayer.
- When hearing an appeal for volunteers who will serve others and sensing an inward drawing to answer the appeal.

- When one is burdened with the hopeless plight of the world's unevangelized population and there arises a sense of call to proclaim the gospel.
- When one is spoken to by an elder in the faith who senses the hand of God upon him or her for leadership.

In whatever manner one may receive his or her call, true spiritual leaders do not serve out of a sense of compulsion or a sense of being driven. Rather, they are drawn to lead by God's Spirit. In God's timing they are brought into the leadership He has chosen for them.

RESPONSE TO THE CALL

It is helpful to observe the responses of some of those whom God called to spiritual leadership in both the Old and New Testaments. The following verses will reveal some responses. Read each passage and record each individual's response to God's call.

Abraham's response—Genesis 12:1–5:

Isaiah's response—Isaiah 6:8, 9:

Moses' response—Exodus 3:1–11, 13; 4:1, 13, 18:

Saul of Tarsus's response—Acts 9:1–20:

Having observed the responses of Abraham, Isaiah, Moses, and Saul of Tarsus to the call of God, write down the following:

Ways in which their responses differ.

Ways in which their responses were similar.

If willingness and obedience are requisite traits for spiritual leadership, on a scale of 1 to 10 (10 being the greatest response)how would you rate Abraham__, Moses__, Isaiah __, and Saul of Tarsus__?

OVERCOMING RELUCTANCE

As you have discovered, Isaiah and Saul of Tarsus seemed to have no problem in immediately obeying God's call. But that was not the case with Moses. His first responses to the call to spiritual leadership were ones of reluctance and excuses. In the following verses list the excuses Moses gave and the ways God responded to them.

Exodus 3	Moses' Excuses	God's Responses
vv. 11, 12		
vv. 13, 14		
Exodus 4		
vv. 1–9		
vv. 10–12		
vv. 13, 14		

WORD WEALTH

The Hebrew words translated "I will certainly be with you" in Exodus 3:12 are identical to those translated "I AM" in verse 14. When God promised Moses that He would be with him, the inference was that He would be a protector and sustainer of His people.

God preferred to be known by the name "I AM WHO I AM" (v. 14) among His people Israel. The name is an expression of His character. He is the dependable and faithful God who is worthy of the full trust of His people.

God patiently dealt with Moses until his fifth and final expression of reluctance, and then He became angry, "So the anger of the Lord was kindled against Moses" (Ex. 4:14). Although the Lord is slow to anger (Ex. 34:6), He does not withhold His anger from His disobedient children forever. However, God's grace toward Moses (Ex. 33:12–16) was greater than His anger toward him, for it was by His grace that God dealt with Moses' reluctance to obey. He assured Moses that He would be with him to enable him to succeed in the great task to which he was called. With that assurance Moses set out, with staff in hand, to do what God had commanded him to do. At last he was obedient to the call.

FAITH ALIVE

Write down any reluctances you may be struggling with that would hinder you from answering the call of God upon your life for spiritual leadership. Next, list steps you plan to take in dealing with your reluctances.

My Reluctances

**Steps I Plan to Take to
Resolve My Reluctances**

If you wish, share these reluctances and ways of dealing with them with a friend. Ask for his or her prayers that you may be freed from those reluctances to stand firmly and respond faithfully to God's call.

 KINGDOM EXTRA

It is helpful to observe the different circumstances in which each of the above men found themselves at the time of the call of God upon their lives. Isaiah, in a vision, saw the Lord's glory when God called him (Is. 6:1–8; John 12:41). Moses was a refugee in a desert place, serving as a shepherd to his father–in–law's flocks (Ex. 2:11–15; 31–10). Saul of Tarsus was on his way to Damascus to arrest believers and bring them bound to Jerusalem (Acts 9:1–15).

Prior to receiving his call, Abraham had been living in Ur of the Chaldeans with his family. He then moved with his father to the city of Haran. The moon god was worshiped in the cities of Ur and Haran, so there was little if anything that would contribute positively to the spiritual life of its inhabitants. Nevertheless, God by His sovereign will called Abraham, "Now the Lord had said to Abram: 'Get out of your country, from your family and from your father's house, to a land that I will show you'" (Gen. 12:1).

From your preceding study, recall Abraham's quick and obedient response, "So Abram departed as the Lord had spoken to him. . . . And Abram was seventy–five years old when he departed from Haran" (Gen. 12:4). Abraham's quick obedience was grounded in faith and this was characteristic of him throughout his life.

It took a willful, conscious decision for Abraham to move out of the comfort zone of family and friends, but he did it. Today the Holy Spirit is calling people to places of spiritual leadership, asking them to leave familiar surroundings, areas of comfort, and familiar routines.

The call may be in surroundings where you are already planted—in your church home or community. But with the world so easily within our reach today because of modern transportation and telecommunications, God's call may lead you to another part of the world, to a different culture and mindset entirely. It is not uncommon for Christians to answer the call by taking vacation time to serve for several weeks or months in ministry in foreign lands. Others in retirement are answering the call to spend extended periods of time in overseas missionary activity.

To whomever the call comes and wherever it may lead, let our response be like that of Abraham—a quick decision to obey. This response will assure that the purposes of God will be fulfilled.

 FAITH ALIVE

Do you fear the unknown? Do you struggle with the thought that God may ask you to leave your comfort zone, leave your loved ones? Or do you feel that because you were not raised in a Christian home with proper religious training, you could never fulfill God's call for your life?

Take a moment to reflect on Abraham's background, his call, and his immediate response to the call. Then consider the position of spiritual leadership God may be calling you to. Write a note to the Lord expressing your heart and asking for His help where you may be struggling to respond to His call.

My Note to the Lord

FOLLOW ME: THE CALL TO DISCIPLESHIP

When Jesus set out on His public ministry, one of the first things He did was to call twelve men to be His disciples. When He gave the call, "Follow Me," without exception each of the twelve left what he was doing and followed Him.

The call to follow Jesus also meant a call to discipleship that required that the Twelve come under His leadership. No longer would they independently decide the direction their lives would take. Instead, they would submit to Him with the commitment that where He led they would follow.

WORD WEALTH

The root word for **disciple** is *manthano* (man–*than*–o), which means: to learn, or be taught (Matt. 9:13; 11:29; 24:32); to learn by practice or experience, acquire a custom or habit (Phil. 4:11; 1 Tim. 5:4, 13); to ascertain, be informed (Acts 23:27); to understand, or comprehend (Rev. 14:3).[4]

To be a disciple of Christ is to learn of Him, be taught by Him, learn by practice or experience, and to assist in spreading His doctrine around the world.

FAITH ALIVE

Everyone who comes to Christ is like a diamond in the rough. A diamond does not reflect its true beauty until it has been removed from the rough soil in which it was found and is polished in the hands of a skilled gemologist, mounted in gold or silver, and displayed for all to see. Even so is it with us when we come to Christ. Through the process of discipleship, He cleanses us, polishes us, and sets us as lights in the world, reflectors of His splendor, servants of the Most High God.

List any area in your life that represents a "diamond in the rough."

List steps you can take to submit to Christ's discipleship so that He can "polish" this area in your life.

A school teacher's finest hour is graduation time for his or her students. As the students march into the school auditorium to the strains of "Pomp and Circumstance" and cross the platform to receive their diplomas, it is reward time for the teacher as well as the students. There is a sense of pride in having had a part in assisting students in achieving their goals.

The goal of discipleship is to make us like Christ. "A disciple is not above his teacher, nor a servant above his master. It is enough for a disciple that he be like his teacher, and a servant like his master" (Matt. 10:24, 25). And it is Christ who enables us to achieve the goals He sets for us in life and in service to Him.

The call to discipleship brought dramatic changes to the disciples' lives. As Jesus taught them the principles of the kingdom of God, their relationship with God changed. God, who had been known to them as the great Creator and the God of their fathers now became known to them as their heavenly Father. Their relationship with their fellowman changed as the teachings of Jesus cleansed them from prejudice toward others. Their worldview changed when they realized they were to take the gospel to the world. Even their professions changed as they left their nets to become "fishers of men," or left the tax table to "receive a spiritual harvest" for God's kingdom. Nothing would ever be the same. But all of the changes in their lives would be for the better.

Changes for the better indeed! Little did they realize what great and wonderful things lay in store for them because of their obedience to the call to serve God. Patiently Jesus taught them about His kingdom. As they watched Him minister to the people, they learned that His was a kingdom built upon compassion, forgiveness, and love. After they had grown in their understanding of His ways, He empowered them by His Spirit to go and call others to follow Him. They learned that in His name and by the authority of His Word they had power to minister to others just as they had seen Him do.

FAITH ALIVE

Like the Twelve, you too heard Jesus' call to discipleship. Since you responded to the call, there have no doubt been many changes in your life. The following questions will provide an outlet for addressing some of those changes.

When did your relationship with God change from an impersonal one to that of Heavenly Father and child?

What changes took place with regard to your relationship with your fellowman?

How has your worldview changed?

Did your decision to follow Christ require a change of occupation? If so, how?

In what ways has Jesus equipped you for ministry to others? Describe the ministry you are engaged in presently.

FOUNDATION PEOPLE

The Twelve became known as apostles. Four of them—Peter, Andrew, James, and John—had been fishermen (Matt. 4:18–22). Matthew had been a tax collector (9:9). No occupations are recorded for the others. Later, Matthias was elected to take the place of Judas Iscariot, who had betrayed the Lord (Acts 1:21–26). And Paul, who had been a tentmaker, was added to the apostolate as "one born out of due time" (18:1–3; 1 Cor. 15:8).

Of those who were founding apostles, Paul wrote, "having been built on the foundation of the apostles and prophets, Jesus Christ Himself being the chief cornerstone" (Eph. 2:20). This metaphorical language conveys the idea of a building that is sitting on an unshakable foundation. The apostles and prophets were foundational in the sense that they preached, taught, and delivered the doctrines upon which all church truth stands.

God's voice is calling for leaders today. He is saying, "Whom shall I send, and who will go for Us?" (Is. 6:8). When Jesus said to Matthew the tax collector, "Follow Me," Matthew arose and followed Him (Matt. 9:9). When He said "Follow Me" to a group of fishermen, they also immediately responded by leaving their nets and following Jesus (4:18–22). May those whom God calls to spiritual leadership today be as prompt in their response.

Saul of Tarsus was a dreaded persecutor of the church when he received the call of God. When he encountered Christ on the Damascus Road, his eyes were blinded by the brightness of His glory. Out of that glory came the voice of Jesus, who identified Himself as the one whom Saul was persecuting. Trembling and astonished, Saul asked, "Lord, what do You want me to do?" (Acts 9:1–6). He was ready to obey! Jesus said of Saul, ". . . he is a chosen vessel of Mine to bear My name before Gentiles, kings, and the children of Israel. For I will show him how many things he must suffer for My name's sake" (vv. 15, 16).

Sometimes the call comes to the most unexpected persons, in the most unexpected ways. If God chooses to do so, He will call the educated or the uneducated, the addict or criminal, the professional or unprofessional. Who would have thought that Saul of Tarsus, the persecutor, would become a chosen vessel of the Lord? Let God be God, and let Him choose whom He will for spiritual leadership. Our responsibility is simply to respond when He calls.

1. *The Analytical Greek Lexicon: New Testament* (New York: Harper and Brothers Publishers), 211.
2. Leighton Ford, *Transforming Leadership* (Downer's Grove, IL: InterVarsity Press, 1991), 37.
3. Ibid.
4. *The Analytical Greek Lexicon: New Testament*, 257.

Lesson 2/Sensitivity to God's Promptings

In the *Spirit-Filled Life Bible,* Jamie Buckingham gives the following comment with regard to hearing God, "The godly leader 'hears' God; that is, his or her spirit is tuned to the promptings and lessons of the Holy Spirit."[1]

Peter, who was destined to be a leader among the apostles, gave evidence of being sensitive to the guidance of the Holy Spirit soon after he answered the call to follow Christ. When the disciples were asked by Jesus, "Who do men say that I, the Son of Man, am?", it was Peter who answered, "You are the Christ, the Son of the living God" (Matt. 16:13–16).

How did Peter know this? The Lord Himself gave the answer when He said, "Blessed are you, Simon Bar-Jonah, for flesh and blood has not revealed this to you, but My Father who is in heaven" (v. 17). Buckingham comments with regard to Peter's revelatory knowledge of Christ's identity, "Jesus emphasized that leadership in His church would always lead and be based not on man's ability to reason things out as much as on his readiness and receptivity to hear God through "revelation knowledge," the things that God unfolds by the work of the Holy Spirit (Eph. 1:17, 18; 3:14–19)."[2]

 WORD WEALTH

Revelation, *apokalupto* (a-pok-a-*loop*-to), means: to uncover, or to reveal (Matt. 11:25); pass; to be disclosed (Luke 2:35; Eph. 3:5); to be plainly signified, or distinctly declared (Rom. 1:17, 18); to be set forth, or announced (Gal. 3:23); to be discovered in true character (1 Cor. 3:13); to be manifested, or appear (John 12:38; Rom. 8:18; 2 Thess. 2:3, 6, 8; 1 Pet. 1:5; 5:1).[3]

WORD WEALTH

"Flesh and blood has not revealed this to you, but My Father who is in heaven" (Matt. 16:17). The Greek words **has not revealed** are *ook apekalupsen,* and they indicate that flesh and blood (men) did not uncover or reveal this truth to Peter but the heavenly Father revealed it to him (see *The Amplified New Testament* on this verse), whereas men had varying opinions as to who Christ was, and they were all wrong(!), Peter, by God's revelation, came up with the right answer.

FAITH ALIVE

When did you make your confession that Jesus is the Christ, the Son of the living God? Before making that confession, how did you sense the promptings of the Spirit to do so?

Do you know a believer who, like Peter, seems especially sensitive to the promptings of the Holy Spirit? If so, ask this person as to how he or she developed that sensitivity, so that you might develop it too.

Samuel is a good example of someone who was mentored to help him recognize the voice of the Lord. He was born in answer to his mother's prayers (1 Sam. 1:2, 9–19). He was taken to Shiloh to be trained by Eli the priest while he was very young (vv. 24–28), and he ministered before the Lord while he was yet a child (2:18). He heard the voice of the Lord calling him, but because he was just a boy he did not recognize it as God's voice. Eli realized that it was God speaking, and he helped Samuel to know how to respond (3:1–15). As Samuel matured, he received many revelations from the Lord, and he became a leader in Israel, serving as a prophet (vv. 19–21) and as a judge (7:15, 16).

FAITH ALIVE

Consider how preoccupations with everyday duties and peripheral concerns make us insensitive to the promptings of the Holy Spirit. How can we avoid falling into that trap?

The New Testament gives many examples of people in places of spiritual leadership who were sensitive to God's promptings. Ananias, who lived in Damascus, was one of those persons. The Lord had said to him in a vision that he should go see Saul of Tarsus and lay his hand on him so that he might receive his sight (Acts 9:10–12). Ananias had heard of how Saul had persecuted the Christians at Jerusalem and how he had authority to jail all in Damascus who called upon the name of the Lord (vv. 13, 14). Had Ananias relied upon his human reasoning, he would not have gone, for in so doing he might have exposed himself and others to bitter persecution. Though Ananias was reluctant at first, he knew that the message was from the Lord, and that he must obey (v. 15).

Following the prompting of the Lord, Ananias went to Saul, laid his hands on him, and Saul received his sight and was filled with the Holy Spirit. Then, after spending several days with the disciples at Damascus, Saul commenced preaching Christ the Son of God in the synagogues (vv. 17–20).

DIVINE REVELATION

Paul's greatness as a spiritual leader is revealed in part by his ability to unfold mysteries that had been kept secret since the beginning of time. Yet when writing to the Ephesians, he was careful to credit that ability not to himself but to divine revelation. He wrote, "how that by revelation He made known to me the mystery (as I have briefly written already, by which, when you read, you may understand my knowledge in the mystery of Christ)" (Eph. 3:3, 4). This was true of all who wrote the Scriptures: men were inspired by the Holy Spirit. Paul wrote to Timothy, "All Scripture is given by inspiration of God, and is profitable for doctrine, for reproof, for correction, for instruction in righteousness" (2 Tim. 3:16).

God will lead and direct our steps through divine revelation found in His Word (Ps. 119:105). When our prayer each day is that of verse 18, "Open my eyes, that I may see wondrous things from Your law," then will we be sensitive to God's voice as He speaks to us through His Word. We will discover new and rich truths from familiar or unfamiliar passages that will provide direction and strength to meet the challenges which spiritual leaders face today.

 ## WORD WEALTH

The word for **inspiration of God** in the Greek language is *theopneustos* and literally means "divinely inspired" or "God-breathed." The inference is that the origin of all Scripture transcends human reason or inspiration. It is given by inspiration of God.

 ## FAITH ALIVE

How are you impacted by the declaration that the Scriptures are divinely inspired?

How should this impact the ministry of the spiritual leader?

Do you read Scripture "on the run," or do you take time daily to read and meditate on God's Word?

If your answer was yes to the preceding question as it related to "on the run," consider setting aside a portion of each day to read your Bible so that God may speak to you through His Word.

DEALING WITH CLOSED DOORS

Not only was Paul sensitive to the Holy Spirit when it came to understanding divine mysteries and in writing the Scriptures, he was also sensitive to the Spirit's leading. What do the following passages show about the ways the Holy Spirit directed Paul?

Acts 13:1–3

Acts 15:12–22

Acts 16:6–10

Acts 17:16–34

Acts 19:21; 20:17–24

With regard to the Macedonian call (Acts 16:9) and how it affected Paul's ministry, Jamie Buckingham comments, "On the basis of the dream, Paul altered his direction, and thus exemplifies a trait of Holy Spirit-guided leaders."[4]

FAITH ALIVE

If you have experienced closed doors as you have endeavored to serve the Lord, briefly describe one of those experiences.

After the fact, can you see the wisdom of God in closing the door to you either temporarily or permanently? What was God's reason?

KINGDOM EXTRA

Ananias and Paul were both sensitive to God's promptings through visions. God still speaks to men today through dreams and visions. In explaining the phenomena that accompanied the outpouring of the Holy Spirit on the Day of Pentecost, Peter quoted from Joel's prophecy:

And it shall come to pass in the last days, says God, that I will pour out of My Spirit on all flesh; Your sons and your daughters shall prophesy, Your young men shall see visions, Your old men shall dream dreams (Acts 2:17).

VISION OF AN OPEN DOOR

Early in his apostolic ministry, Peter was given a vision that would play a significant part in how he viewed evangelism. It was a vision of an open door. Although he did not immediately understand the vision, Peter was sensitive to God's promptings and obeyed the Spirit's voice.

FAITH ALIVE

Read Acts 10. What do you understand as the meaning of the vision God gave to Peter? (vv. 7–16, 28)

Why do you think Peter struggled with the message of the vision? (vv. 17, 19)

How would you have responded?

What can you learn from Peter's affirmative response to the Holy Spirit?

Has God ever spoken to you through a vision? What was your response?

To what extent do you share Peter's vision of reaching the lost through your ministry?

 ## KINGDOM EXTRA

If the Spirit is to be poured out on all flesh with the accompanying supernatural manifestations listed in Acts 2:17, it stands to reason that those in places of leadership should be among the recipients.

Review the accounts in the Book of Acts of the outpouring of the Holy Spirit on the following groups:

The believers on the Day of Pentecost—2:1–4
The Samaritans—8:14–17
Cornelius and his company—10:34–46
The Ephesians—19:1–7

In the above events (except Pentecost), when believers received the gift of the Holy Spirit, individuals were used to minister the gift to other believers. At Samaria, Peter and John laid hands on the recipients. Peter was preaching when Cornelius received the gift. Paul laid his hands on believers at Ephesus and they received it.

In the light of these accounts, two questions present themselves (write down your answer to each question):

Question 1—Did I receive the Spirit when I believed (or thereafter)?

Question 2—If I have received the Spirit, how am I being used of the Lord to encourage other believers to receive the Spirit too?

WORD OF WISDOM AND WORD OF KNOWLEDGE

The promptings of God can come through the Holy Spirit gifts of the word of wisdom and the word of knowledge (1 Cor. 12:7, 8). "The word of wisdom is a spiritual utterance at a given moment through the Spirit, supernaturally disclosing the mind, purpose, and way of God as applied to a specific situation. The word of knowledge is a supernatural revelation of information pertaining to a person or an event, given for a specific purpose, usually having to do with an immediate need"[5]

Often a leader faces situations where decisions must be made and there is no possible way, in the natural, to receive all the facts or information needed to make the right decision or to give the proper advice. This is when the gift of the word of wisdom or the word of knowledge can play an important role. The Holy Spirit exercises these gifts through anointed leadership to give them special insights into the situation. Practical wisdom comes through past experiences. But practical wisdom in itself is not always sufficient for the complex needs of people today. Wisdom that comes from the Spirit is also needed.

Read the following passages to discover examples of revelatory knowledge or wisdom. Write a brief statement about its use in each situation.

2 Kings 5:20–27

John 4:1–18.

Acts 15:1–31

 FAITH ALIVE

In your own words, define the following two gifts:

Word of Wisdom

Word of Knowledge

Recall a time when you first observed or experienced either of these gifts in action and describe the results or response to their usage.

Describe the importance of these gifts in your ministry now, or perhaps a ministry you are anticipating in the near future.

PROMPTINGS OF THE HOLY SPIRIT

God's promptings come in a variety of ways: through the written Word, through closed and opened doors, through the prophets, and through spiritual gifts. And we can add to those the promptings of the blessed Holy Spirit who dwells within believers.

 AT A GLANCE

In this study you have considered several biblical passages where the Holy Spirit was at work speaking to and guiding church leaders in the work of the ministry. Read the following passages and record after each one the person, the Holy Spirit's promptings to that person, and the result of obedience to His promptings.

Bible Reference	Person	Holy Spirit's Prompting	Result of Obedience
Luke 2:25–35			
4:1–13			

Bible Reference	Person	Holy Spirit's Prompting	Result of Obedience
Acts 8:26–39			
18:5, 6			

As you discovered, when we obey the Holy Spirit's promptings things begin to happen! We become His instruments to accomplish God's plans and purposes in building His kingdom. And in the process, He is building in us leadership qualities that will make us strong enough to meet the challenges of today.

 FAITH ALIVE

Can you remember a time when the Holy Spirit spoke to you, but at the time you thought it was your own thoughts so ignored His promptings? If so, record here what you learned from the experience.

List unusual times (and perhaps locations) when the Holy Spirit spoke to you. Record the results that occurred as you were obedient.

If you are finding it difficult to be sensitive to the Holy Spirit's promptings, ask a friend to pray with you about it. God wants you to enjoy the fellowship of the Spirit and to be led by Him.

It is imperative that the spiritual leader be sensitive to the promptings of the Spirit. Reliance upon human reasoning alone will not get the work of God done. Let us heed the word of the prophet Zechariah, "'Not by might nor by power, but by My Spirit,' says the Lord of hosts" (Zech. 4:6).

1. *Spirit-Filled Life Bible* (Nashville, TN: Thomas Nelson Publishers, 1991), 1436, "Kingdom Dynamics: Matt. 16:13–20, Hearing God."

2. Ibid.

3. *The Analytical Greek Lexicon: New Testament* (New York: Harper and Brothers Publishers), 42.

4. *Spirit-Filled Life Bible*, 1658, "Kingdom Dynamics: Acts 16:6–10, Dreams and Visions."

5. Ibid., 1736, note on 1 Cor. 12:8–11.

Lesson 3/Demonstrating an Exemplary Christian Life-style

THE HIGH STANDARD FOR LEADERSHIP

"My brethren, let not many of you become teachers, knowing that we shall receive a stricter judgment" (James 3:1).

In this verse James lets those in places of spiritual leadership know that they will be held accountable for exemplifying Jesus Christ in their personal lives as well as their ministry duties. Spiritual leaders are judged first of all by what they exemplify in character. They are judged by what they are, first, and then by what they do. It has to do with the condition of a leader's heart and spirit more than with the person's achievements.

If you were asked to name seven qualifications for Christian leadership, what qualifications would your list include? Give a reason why you listed each.

Seven Qualifications for Christian Leadership	Reason for Selection
1.	
2.	
3.	

Seven Qualifications for Christian Leadership	Reason for Selection
4.	
5.	
6.	
7.	

Our lists of qualifications for leadership will probably vary. We all have ideas as to what a leader should be like. But who is a man or woman of God? How can we recognize him or her?

These questions needed answers in the early church too. Both Timothy and Titus, leaders in the early church, were faced with these questions. Can you imagine starting at square one, as they had to do, and having to appoint overseers in the churches? Apparently there were people who had a desire to teach, preach, administrate, or serve in various capacities. But what criteria were available to them by which to determine a person's eligibility to serve in the church? Was there a professionally prepared profile by which to measure a potential leader? If Timothy and Titus had each prepared lists of qualifications for leadership, as we did in the preceding exercise, their lists would probably have had some differences too, and they probably needed help in making leadership appointments.

That help came in the letters they received from the apostle Paul. In 1 Timothy 3:1–7 and in Titus 1:5–9, he provided for them, and for us, the profile needed for testing spiritual maturity or spiritual qualifications for leadership.

The lists found in 1 Timothy and Titus can be combined as follows:

1. Blameless

2. The husband of one wife

3. Temperate

4. Sober-minded

5. Of good behavior

6. Hospitable

7. Able to teach

8. Not given to wine

9. Not violent

10. Not greedy for money

11. Gentle

12. Not quarrelsome

13. Not covetous

14. One who rules his own house well with his children in submission

15. Not a novice

16. Has a good testimony among those who are outside

17. Not self-willed

18. Not quick-tempered

19. Lover of what is good

20. Responsible steward

21. Just

22. Holy

23. Self–controlled

24. Holds fast to the Word

Write your thoughts as to the meaning of each of the above in the space under it. Having done that, you may feel that no one can fulfill such a high standard! Since it is a growth process, I can rejoice in the good things Christ produces in me, while at the same time trusting His love and grace when I don't measure up as well as I should.

 WORD WEALTH

The Greek word for **desire** in 1 Timothy 3:1 is *orego,* which means: to extend, stretch one's self out, to reach forward to, to desire earnestly, long after.

The Greek word for **bishop** is *episkopos,* which is used to designate the pastoral position in a local church. Other words used by the apostle Paul to designate the same office are "presbyter" and "elder."

FAITH ALIVE

What importance would you place on the element of "desire" on the part of one who aspires to become a leader in the church?

CRITERIA FOR ALL BELIEVERS

Though the twenty-four characteristics listed in the 1 Timothy and Titus passages appear to be the norm for leaders today, they are also qualities that all followers of Christ should desire and strive for. Most of the twenty-four characteristics are applied to all Christians in Paul's other New Testament letters.

The idea that all believers should strive for this high standard seems to be strengthened by the following passage in 1 Timothy 3:8–12 that deals with the qualifications for deacons and their wives:

> Likewise deacons must be reverent, not double-tongued, not given to much wine, not greedy for money, holding the mystery of the faith with a pure conscience. But let these first be tested; then let them serve as deacons, being found blameless. Likewise, their wives must be reverent, not slanderers, temperate, faithful in all things. Let deacons be the husbands of one wife, ruling their children and their own houses well.

"The dominant idea among NT leaders was that the ministry belonged to the whole believing community."[1] This could imply that the spiritual qualities under consideration here would be expected to appear in some degree in each believer's life. Further, if mature believers were sought out for leadership roles, they could only be found in such a community.

A CLOSER LOOK AT BIBLICAL QUALIFICATIONS

   KINGDOM EXTRA

With the aid of a study Bible, commentary, Greek lexicon, or other resource materials, discover the expanded meanings of the words and phrases used in 1 Timothy 3:2–7. The following questions will assist you in your discovery.

v. 2: Does the word "blameless" imply perfection? If not, what does it mean?

What does "the husband of one wife" imply? Does this mean the spiritual leader cannot be single? Not divorced? Not widowed? Not remarried? Not a polygamist?

vv. 2, 3: List the positive and negative traits found in these verses.

Positive   Negative

vv. 4, 5: Why is it so important for the spiritual leader to have success in managing his home?

v. 6: What are the dangers inherent in appointing a new convert as an overseer of the church?

v. 7: Of what value to the spiritual leader is a good reputation in the community?

In 1 Timothy 1:3–7, 4:1–3, and 6:3–5, the apostle Paul deals with the problem of false teachers. False teachers are characterized in these verses as lacking understanding, apostate from the faith, deceptive, liars, hypocrites, without conscience, proud, knowing nothing, corrupt minds, and so on. Perhaps this problem prompted him to stipulate the qualifications of a true spiritual leader in 1 Timothy 3:2–7.

Paul's emphasis is more on "being" than on "doing" when he addresses the issue of qualifications for spiritual leadership. "What you are speaks so loud that I can't hear what you say," is an old saying that bears much truth.

FAITH ALIVE

What is distinctly Christian about the qualifications in 1 Timothy when compared to those one would find in the corporate world?

Of these qualities that are desirable for spiritual leadership, list the ones you feel are strengths in your life.

List those you need to develop or improve. What steps will you take to make those improvements?

KINGDOM EXTRA

With regard to character qualifications, "There are over a dozen significant qualities expected, which include spiritual preparedness, self-control, social graciousness, domestic order, and holy living. The basis for continual ministry is continual commitment to character. If a leader falls from these ethical standards, he or she should accept removal from leadership until an appropriate season of reverifying of character can be fulfilled (Gal. 6:1, 2)."[2]

 FAITH ALIVE

Now that you have considered the biblical qualifications for leaders, compare those with the seven qualifications you listed at the beginning of this chapter's study. How does your list measure up to the biblical list? What adjustments must you make, if any?

HONESTY: THE FIRST–RANKING CHARACTERISTIC

The quality of "honesty" is not listed by that name on the list we have considered thus far, though it is implied. But because of its prominence on the list of expectations of those in places of leadership in the business world, I give it special mention here.

In their book, *The Leadership Challenge,* James M. Kouzes and Barry Z. Posner give the results of a survey they made of 2,600 top-level managers, whom they asked to complete a checklist of superior leadership characteristics. According to their research, at the top of a list of twenty superior leadership characteristics was honesty.[3]

Honesty is also one of the prime characteristics one would expect to find in the spiritual leader. Honesty includes the idea of being truthful, trustworthy, ethical, and principled. A true spiritual leader evidences honesty by practicing what he or she preaches and teaches.

THREE OTHER CHARACTERISTICS

Discover and list the three required characteristics for the seven men who were to be selected by the early church to serve as deacons (Acts 6:3).

1.

2.

3.

WORD WEALTH

The Greek word for **good reputation** in Acts 6:3 is *marturouminos*. The same word appears in Acts 10:22 in reference to the Roman centurion, Cornelius. It was said of Cornelius that he was a man of good reputation among the Gentiles. The *King James Version* translates *marturouminos* as "honest report" in Acts 6:3 and "good report" in Acts 10:22. The underlying meaning of *marturouminos* is "attestation to character."

KINGDOM EXTRA

The requirements for the seven deacons included being "full of the Holy Spirit and wisdom." Read the following verses and use your study Bible and a commentary to gain additional insight to being full of the Holy Spirit and wisdom. In your exploration of these scriptures, you will discover the importance of the two following requirements for spiritual leaders.

**Full of the
Holy Spirit**

Gen. 41:38; Acts 1:8; 2:4;
4:8, 31; 6:5; 7:55; 8:14, 15,
17; 9:17; 10:38; 11:22–24

Full of Wisdom

Ex. 31:6; 1 Kin. 4:29;
Ps. 51:6; Prov. 2:6; 16:16;
Luke 2:52; Acts 7:9, 10;
1 Cor. 12:7, 8; Col. 1:9, 28;
James 1:5

"Leadership in the church must be full of both the Holy Spirit and wisdom. The Holy Spirit gives us God's perspective. Wisdom is the practical side of problem solving."[4]

FAITH ALIVE

Describe in a few sentences what you understand to be the meaning of the phrase "full of the Holy Spirit."

What is your understanding of being "full of . . . wisdom"?

Which of the three qualifications for the selection of the seven deacons seems to have been preeminent in making the selection, and why do you suppose it was so?

A CASE OF DISHONESTY IN THE EARLY CHURCH

The believers in the early church shared in all things. All who owned lands or houses sold them and brought the proceeds and laid them at the apostles' feet. Then they distributed to each as anyone had need. In the midst of this, Acts 5:1–11 describes the lack of honesty in the lives of Ananias and Sapphira. They had sold a possession; but they chose not to give all they had received.

Read Acts 5:1–11 and note:

1. What exactly was the beginning of this sin? (v. 2)

2. Does Peter say they "had" to give everything? (v. 4a)

3. If keeping part was their privilege, then what was their essential sin? (v. 46)

"Ananias and Sapphira were judged for their hypocrisy and lying to God, not for their decision to retain some of their personal property for themselves (Acts 5:4). The severity of the punishment for such a small offense may seem intolerant and graceless (see Luke 9:54, 55), but it was necessary both to establish apostolic authority in the early church and to safeguard the church's purity. A sobering lesson is that Satan has the power to distort the thinking of Christians (v. 3), thus affirming our need to allow him no place (Eph. 4:27)."[5]

The believer's best defense against self-deception is through mutual accountability to one another (especially to a local congregation, Eph. 5:21). Final renewing of the mind through the Word and a sustained "fullness" of the Holy Spirit are also safeguards. Read Romans 12:1, 2; 2 Corinthians 10:4, 5; and Ephesians 5:17–20, and note your impression of what your response to these passages should be in seeking to maintain personal integrity.

 FAITH ALIVE

Do you have a problem with honesty in your life? If so, put a check in front of the following listed area(s) where you struggle with this attribute.

__ Finances __ Spouse/other Family Members
__ Ministry __ Work __ Friends __ College
__ Other _____

Seek God earnestly to help you to overcome dishonesty in your life. He is willing to forgive you and make you strong where you are weak.

Write down the name of a mature believer to whom you can go for prayer support and counsel. Perhaps it is this person to whom you can be accountable in the areas in which you are struggling.

Now rate yourself on the second and third qualifications that were required of the seven deacons in the early church. Put a check in the appropriate column.

	Always	Most of the Time	Sometimes
Full of the Holy Spirit			
Full of Wisdom			

How can you strengthen the areas in which you are weak? List the steps you plan to take to accomplish this.

Remember that character growth is a process. Maturity will come moment by moment, day by day, experience after experience, through daily submission to God's Word and through abiding in the fullness of His Spirit, until you become the kind of person who possesses these characteristics.

1. *Spirit-Filled Life Bible* (Nashville, TN: Thomas Nelson Publishers, 1991), 1844, "Kingdom Dynamics: 1 Tim. 3:1–13, Character Qualifications."
2. Ibid.
3. James M. Kouzes and Barry Z. Posner, *The Leadership Challenge* (San Francisco: Jossey-Bass Publishers, 1987), 16–17.
4. *Spirit-Filled Life Bible*, 1635, note on Acts 6:3.
5. Ibid., 1633, note on Acts 5:1–11.

Lesson 4/Humility, Willingness, and Total Commitment

HUMILITY

To understand Jesus is to understand humility. Jesus is humility personified. In His preincarnate glory, He was equal with God and was the Creator of the world. In His incarnation He came down from His glory and was born as a human being. When he grew up, He humbled Himself further and became a servant, going about teaching, healing, and working miracles. He came not to be ministered to but to minister, to be a servant.

Since we have never been to heaven, we cannot possibly understand the magnitude of the change that took place when Christ became a man: when the Creator took upon himself the likeness of the creature; when He left the glories of heaven and came down to the darkness of the earth; when He left the serenity of an environment where the will of God is done and there is no sin and came to an earth that is ravaged by rebellion and sin.

A couple who served as missionaries in Papua New Guinea brought a delegation of Papuan believers to the United States to attend their denomination's annual convention. On a day when they were touring the city where the convention was being held, they took the group to a supermarket. As they passed through the produce area, the lady missionary noticed that one of the Papuan pastors was weeping. Concerned that something was wrong, she inquired as to the reason for his tears. He responded, "Only now am I realizing how many comforts you and your family left behind in order to take the gospel to us in Papua New Guinea."

It is true. Every missionary who leaves the comforts of home, family, and friends to take the gospel to other lands pays a great price. But it cannot begin to compare with the great price Christ paid by leaving heaven to come to earth to redeem humankind.

There is much talk today about upward mobility. Everyone wants it. Yet Christ demonstrated downward mobility. He came down to earth to serve the needs of the people, even to death on the Cross to make atonement for our sins.

Jesus set the example for all who would follow Him in ministry. There was nothing self-serving about Him. His thoughts and prayers were for the people.

1. What does Matthew 11:28, 29 show us about Jesus' concern for people?

2. Read Matthew 9:36–38. What do these words of Jesus speak to you about His call on your caring heart for others?

In his letter to the Philippian church, the apostle Paul appealed to the believers to serve each other in humility by following Christ's example.

> Let nothing be done through selfish ambition or conceit, but in lowliness of mind let each esteem others better than himself. Let each of you look out not only for his own interests, but also for the interests of others. Let this mind be in you which was also in Christ Jesus, who being in the form of God, did not consider it robbery to be equal with God, but made Himself of no reputation, taking the form of a bond-servant, and coming in the likeness of men (Phil. 2:3–7).

WORD WEALTH

Made Himself of no reputation comes from the Greek word *ekenesen,* which means to divest one's self of one's prerogatives, abase one's self, to empty one's self of one's privileges.

Read the following verses and describe how Christ's humility was demonstrated.

Matthew 11:29

Luke 2:7

John 13:5

Philippians 2:8

In his book, *Descending into Greatness,* Bill Hybels comments on the humility described in Philippians 2.

> Simply stated, the message of Philippians is this: If you want to be truly great, then the direction you must go is down. You must descend into greatness. At the heart of this paradox is still another paradox: Greatness is not a measure of self-will, but rather self-abandonment. The more you lose, the more you gain.[1]

Many lessons can also be learned from Bible people in the Old and New Testaments. Both men and women (not all leaders) demonstrated humility as they faced different situations and tests in their lives. Read the following Scripture passages and then enter a short statement after each reference, describing how humility was demonstrated in each situation.

Gideon—Judges 6:11–15

Ruth—Ruth 2:1–12

David—2 Samuel 6:12–22

1 Chronicles 17:1–19

Josiah—2 Chronicles 34:1–3

Mary—Luke 1:26–31; 46–49

Elizabeth—Luke 1:39–43

Tax Collector—Luke 18:9–14

 FAITH ALIVE

Do you know anyone toward whom you feel superior? Though it may be difficult to do so, write down the reasons why you feel that way toward this person.

What truth from Philippians 2:3–7 can help you overcome your feeling of superiority?

Do you look out for the interests of others? How can you show more interest to those in your 1) home; 2) community; 3) church; 4) workplace?

List the area(s) in your life where it is difficult to take a humble posture (e.g. in a relationship, a position of employment, or being accountable to someone else). Ask God to strengthen you and give you grace in this area(s) so that you might be a leader who serves in a spirit of humility.

WILLINGNESS

Willingness is a desirable trait for spiritual leadership. Peter saw the importance of it when he wrote, "Shepherd the flock of God which is among you, serving as overseers not by compulsion but willingly [emphasis added], not for dishonest gain but eagerly" (1 Pet. 5:2).

 WORD WEALTH

Willingly comes from the Greek word *ekousios,* which means "voluntarily," or "spontaneously."

David was a man who served God willingly and wholeheartedly. God was pleased with David's attitude toward Him, and He commended David by saying that he was "a man after His own heart" (1 Sam. 13:14).

When David's reign over Israel was drawing to a close, Solomon his son was chosen to succeed him as king. What counsel did David give Solomon from 1 Chronicles 28:9? This is good advice for all who serve the Lord and lead others.

To try to serve God unwillingly creates great stress in one's life. I know of a woman who was serving in a very responsible position in a school that trained Christian leaders. When her health began to fail, she went to a clinic and underwent an extensive physical examination. The findings of the examination were surprising. There was nothing physically wrong with the woman. It was determined that her problem was stress.

The doctor asked what it was that would bring such stress in her life. Her response was a surprise to herself as well as to the doctor. She told him she was not happy with the work she was doing, but because of circumstances that she felt were beyond her control, she had no choice but to serve. Though she served faithfully and efficiently, she did not tell anyone of the inward struggle she was having. To do so, in her thinking, would be wrong. As a result, the inner conflict was ruining her health.

It is of great importance that we find the position of ministry that God has for us, and then serve wholeheartedly and willingly in that position. Instead of stress, we will experience joy in God's service and He will be pleased.

Jesus demonstrated the epitome of willingness in ministry to the Father. He willingly became a servant, a man, and He willingly gave Himself in untiring ministry to others. In His greatest stress, what did Jesus say (Matthew 26:36–44)? Christ's willingness went "all the way." He calls us that far too.

 FAITH ALIVE

Read Matthew 26:36–45.

Jesus' disciples were willing to stand watch in prayer in Gethsemane, but their willingness was overcome by human fatigue. What did Jesus observe? (v. 41)

This is our problem as well; though willing to serve the Lord, our flesh is often weak. What in Jesus' counsel offers us answers?

Willingness will win out in our lives as we learn to walk in the Spirit, by His power overcoming the weakness of the flesh. Jot down the areas in your life where you identify with the disciples, finding your flesh to be weak.

Now be more specific and note a situation where you deeply desired to do what you knew God wanted you to do, but you failed to fulfill the task in spite of your good intentions.

Is there an area in your ministry in which you are not serving willingly and, as a result, are experiencing stress? Write down your thoughts about the situation and how you plan to deal with it.

Check any one of the following areas that may strengthen your willingness to serve:

__Commitment __Prayer   __Self-Discipline

__Priorities   __Avoiding Overload __Counsel

Now get more specific. Which two are areas where you know you can give the most?

List any barriers or challenges you see to growing in each area.

Counting on God's resources, what actions will you commit to for at least one month to stimulate your growth?

 FAITH ALIVE

We all serve in a leadership role in some way. Write down how you perceive yourself measuring up to Peter's leadership standard as it is recorded in 1 Peter 5:1–11. What are your strong areas? your weak areas?

How do you test your motives in your ministry to God? Does the end justify the means?

How would you relate this passage (1 Pet. 5:1–11) to 1 Corinthians 3:11–15?

TOTAL COMMITMENT

The apostle Paul was totally committed to the call of God. After sharing the testimony of his glorious vision of Christ and his conversion, what was Paul's concluding observation, which helps to explain his effective life for Christ (see Acts 26:19)?

That Paul was totally committed and obedient to the heavenly vision even during times of bitter persecution is borne out in the following scriptures. Read the passages and then write down the groups of people who opposed him and the persecution or threats Paul experienced in each instance. (Note that none of these deterred him from fulfilling the call of God on his life.)

Acts	Location	Opposition	Persecution/ Threat
9:22–25			
9:28–30			
14:1–5			
14:6, 19, 20			

Paul was committed to reach all the cultures where God had called him. To the Corinthians he wrote, "For though I am free from all men, I have made myself servant to all, that I might win the more" (1 Cor. 9:19). In the following verses found in 1 Corinthians 9, list the ways in which Paul adapted himself to various people and situations:

Verse 20

Verse 21

Verse 22

When Paul wrote in verse 20 that he became as a Jew and as one under the Law, he was not compromising. Acts 16:1–3 exemplifies this. Read the passage and note how adaptability is illustrated.

> Paul, the chief spokesman of salvation by grace alone, had the half-Jewish Timothy circumcised so that he could take him into the Jewish synagogues. This was not compromise; it was simple Christian courtesy. It was a mature recognition that social, cultural, and even religious differences should never become more important issues than the simple message of salvation in Christ.[2]

Although Paul was the apostle of the Gentiles, he did not excuse himself from complying with the Jewish traditions if it meant he could influence the Jews to receive salvation through Christ. In contrast, what do we find in Galatians 2:1–5?

In 1 Corinthians 9:20–22 Paul declares his flexible policy. He had Timothy, who was half–Jewish, to be circumcised so as not to offend the Jews, and thus to open the door to reach them with the gospel. But he refused to have Titus, a Greek, circumcised just to please the leaders of the Jerusalem church. To Paul this act would have been a compromise, setting a precedent that could result in others falling from the gospel's grace into legalistic bondage. (For other examples read Galatians 1:6 and 3:1–9.)

When Paul said, "To the weak I became as weak" (1 Cor. 9:22), he was referring to those believers who were weak in their faith. Read Romans 14 and complete the following exercise.

In your own words describe a "weak" brother or sister in this sense.

What should be our attitude toward a "weak" believer?

In the end, who will be our final judge?

List the two things we are told in verse 13 not to do.

1.

2.

What do you understand as the meaning of verse 20?

What does verse 21 teach about being sensitive toward others who may be weak in the faith? (Some refer to this verse as being the "law of Christian liberty," e.g., "I can, but I will not if it is offensive to a fellow Christian.")

Paul did not despise nor judge the weak but became as one of them, so as not to put a stumbling block before them. He refused to use his liberty if it would cause a weak believer to fall from the gospel into heathen idolatry.

Though Paul was a freeborn Roman citizen (not a slave, nor one who purchased his citizenship, Acts 22:25–28), and though he was not dependent upon anyone for his subsistence, he was willing to become a servant that others might become free. His total commitment to Christ led him to willingly adapt himself as much as possible to all groups, he says, "that I might by all means save some" (1 Cor. 9:22). "Without violating biblical morality, he would go to any length to enter the world of others and lead them to salvation."[3] In this way, Paul's commitment to reach as many as possible with the gospel is a model of Christian leadership for us.

 FAITH ALIVE

In your own words describe how you may "become all things to all men" in order to win people to Christ.

Are there groups of people in your community who are not being reached with the gospel? The homeless? Unwed mothers? Homosexuals? Minority groups? Older people in convalescent homes? Children? List some of the fears or prejudices that you may feel could hinder your ministry to any one of these groups.

Pray specifically about these prejudices or fears, asking God for His help and strength to overcome. Read Matthew 25:31–40, John 4:18, 1 Corinthians 12:9, and Philippians 4:13.

What criticism might you encounter if you tried to reach one of the aforementioned groups? How could this lesson help you to deal with such criticism?

Consider how you may become "all things to all men" by entering the world of others who are closer to home. For example, family members, co-workers, neighbors, friends.

List the steps you can take to reach at least one of the above groups with the gospel.

 FAITH ALIVE

Christ calls each of us to total commitment today—total commitment to serve humbly and willingly. The harvest still needs to be brought in. The sheep still need shepherds. All kinds of people need to hear the gospel, some for the first time. Read Romans 12:1 and 2, and then write out a prayer of total commitment to the Lord.

1. Bill Hybels, *Descending into Greatness* (Grand Rapids, MI: Zondervan Publishing House, 1993), 16–17. Used by permission.

2. *Spirit-Filled Life Bible* (Nashville, TN: Thomas Nelson Publishers, 1991), 1657, note on Acts 16:3.

3. Ibid., 1731, note on 1 Cor. 9:19–23.

Lesson 5/ Ministering with Confidence

The place was Los Angeles, California. The occasion was the gathering of thousands of people in a large church building located in the heart of the city. They had come to hear an evangelist who had been called to conduct a two-week evangelistic crusade that was designed to reach the Greater Los Angeles area.

After an inspiring time of worship and special music, the host pastor introduced the speaker. Quiet fell over the congregation, and there was an atmosphere of expectancy as he stepped forward to the podium.

There was reason enough for this atmosphere of expectancy, for great things had been happening during the crusade. Night after night most of the seats in the church's auditorium had been filled with people eager to hear the speaker's sermons. And now, as the crusade moved into its third week, it was no different. What was intended to be a two-week crusade extended into the third and fourth weeks, so successful were the meetings.

It was because of the amazing move of the Holy Spirit that the meetings had been extended. Hundreds had made decisions for Christ. Some gave testimony to Holy Spirit infilling, while others spoke of receiving healing for their bodies and even visions of glory.

Who was this man whom God had so mightily used? Why did so any people respond to his ministry? Though he will go unnamed, I am qualified to describe him to you, for your writer was one of those who made a decision for Christ during the crusade.

It was not because of his charisma that he had such success, though he was pleasant and winsome. It was not because he was flashy or flamboyant, though he was well-dressed and well-groomed. It wasn't because he was eloquent of speech, though he was an excellent communicator. It was something else that came across as he ministered the Word. It was his confidence that fairly exuded from his message and his demeanor.

It was obvious that this man was confident of God's call upon his life and confident that he had been commissioned to preach the gospel. As the people listened, they became aware that he was totally focused on doing the thing God had called him to do, and that was to bring people to Christ. His confidence was so great that it spilled over on the people, and they began to reach out to their families and friends to bring them to the crusade meetings.

Confidence was also reflected in the man's message. He was fully persuaded of the power of the gospel to bring salvation to all who believe. His confidence was especially revealed when he addressed controversial issues without fear or favor. Instead of driving people away, this brought favorable responses from them, for they wanted to hear the truth.

Confidence was also a reflection of the many years he had lived the victorious Christian life. Conversion in childhood and an upbringing in the church through his formative years had instilled in him a great confidence and trust in God.

Something about the man let you know that had he undertaken almost any other profession he would have been successful. But his response to the call of God early in his life eliminated any other professional options. He continued to minister around the world for many years and did not die until he was over ninety years of age. Being such a model of confidence, no doubt he had gained strength many times from reading the following words of Scripture, "Therefore do not cast away your confidence, which has great reward" (Heb. 10:35).

   WORD WEALTH

Confidence, *parrhesia;* means all outspokenness, i.e., frankness, bluntness; by implication; assurance; confidence; "if we hold fast the confidence" (Heb.3:6).[1] The Greek definition of confidence implies not just a strong persuasion of what we believe, but a bold stance of faith in everything we do, think, and speak.

CONFIDENCE:
THE RESULT OF A GOOD RELATIONSHIP WITH GOD

A seminar speaker who was addressing a group of pastors and their wives caught their attention when he said, "You need a God you can live with comfortably, and there is One such God—the Living God. For one to be comfortable with God, you must have a good relationship with Him, and for such a relationship to exist, you will need a clear understanding of His true nature."

There is little chance that a good relationship with God will become a reality if He is perceived to be a perpetually "angry" God who can never be pleased, or Someone who assigns impossible tasks, or who vindictively punishes every small mistake. The seminar speaker went on to say, "Such a vindictive view of God produces sick, neurotic spiritual leaders. They in turn produce sick, neurotic followers. People suffer from the diseases we give them."[2]

On the other hand, when God is accurately perceived as the Lord of infinite love, abundant in grace, instant in forgiveness to the penitent, and absolutely faithful to those who put their trust in Him, a good and loving relationship will result. Such a relationship with God will produce great confidence.

   FAITH ALIVE

Upon what do you base your perceptions of God?

What part does the Bible play in forming your perceptions of Him?

Who are the people who have influenced you most in your understanding of God?

How would you describe your relationship with God? Comfortable? Distant? Good? Strained? Why?

When do you experience the greatest confidence in your walk with the Lord?

List the things that seem to contribute to that confidence.

What part does Bible study, prayer, and Christian fellowship play in your confidence?

CONFIDENCE:
THE RESULT OF A SENSE OF PERSONAL IDENTITY

Leighton Ford writes, "A sense of identity, a security that comes from knowing who one is, lies at the heart of leadership. Leadership is first of all not something one does but something one is. This comes out clearly in the story of Jesus when his Father affirms him as his special son (Matt. 3:17; Mark 1:11; Luke 3:22). Jesus operated out of a sense of quiet confidence that came from knowing who he was in his everlasting relationship with his Father."[3]

Jesus displayed the psychological security essential to be a servant-leader. This security was demonstrated when He washed His disciples' feet. Read John 13:1–7, and after reflecting upon it, write down your answer to the following question.

How is Jesus' confidence in His self-identity revealed in verses 1 and 3?

The servant leader leads from a position of personal security, that is, knowing who God has made him or her to be, and resting in the peaceful awareness and confidence that God's hand is ordering his or her personal destiny. The godly leader is one who stoops to help another. . . . Until a person is ready to wash feet he is not qualified to be a kingdom leader.[4]

 FAITH ALIVE

How would you have felt had you been one of the disciples and Jesus came to you and knelt down before you to wash your feet?

Would you have understood why Jesus could do this, or would you have reacted as did Peter? Give a reason for your response.

How did Jesus challenge His disciples then, and how does He challenge us now with the idea of what it means to be a servant leader?

CONFIDENCE:
THE RESULT OF KNOWING ONE'S GIFTING

Jesus is the supreme example of one who possessed complete confidence in leadership. He knew who He was, the Christ, the Son of the living God. He knew why He had come into the world. He also knew how He had been gifted and equipped by the Father to accomplish His mission on earth.

Read the passages listed below. How do they reveal Jesus' awareness of His giftedness for spiritual leadership?

Luke 4:18, 19 (cf. Is. 61:1–3)

Spiritual gifts are available to all believers to equip them for ministry. The Bible clearly teaches that Christians are to serve God with these spiritual gifts. The following passages provide a comprehensive list of the spiritual gifts.

List the spiritual gifts mentioned in Romans 12:6–8, and note the manner in which each gift is to be ministered; e.g., if prophecy, let us prophesy in proportion to our faith.

What gifts are found in 1 Corinthians 12:28 that were not included in the list of Romans 12:6–8?

How does the list of spiritual gifts in Ephesians 4:11, 12 compare to the previous two? How is the church to be benefited by these spiritual gifts?

Distinct among the vast spectrum of spiritual gifts, the Holy Spirit's gifts are given as a resource He distributes at His will, enabling special, supernatural manifestations to be available through all believers, at His time and in His way. List these gifts from 1 Corinthians 12:8–10.

Love is the greatest gift of all. List the characteristics of love that are found in 1 Corinthians 13:4–8.

Being aware of spiritual gifts creates confidence in spiritual leaders. Knowing God appoints and enables, let us take the necessary steps to discover what gifts we possess. *The Amplified Bible* puts 1 Corinthian 14:1 this way, "Eagerly pursue and seek to acquire love—make it your aim, your great quest; and earnestly desire and cultivate the spiritual endowments, especially that you may prophesy—that is, interpret the divine will and purpose in inspired preaching and teaching."

CONFIDENCE:
THE RESULT OF STUDY AND TRAINING

Jesus was the exception when it came to the need for attending a Bible college or seminary before being ordained to the ministry. On one occasion after He had taught in the temple, "the Jews marvelled, saying, 'How does this man know letters, having never studied?'" (John 7:14, 15). "*Letters* refers not to the basic ability of reading and writing, but to Jesus' knowledge and understanding of the Scriptures. Their puzzlement was over Jesus' extraordinary knowledge without having . . . studied at one of the prestigious and official rabbinic schools of Shammai and Hillel."[5]

Jesus did not need Bible college or seminary training, simply because He was the Word of God incarnate. But for those who would lead others today, there is no substitute for becoming rooted and grounded in the Bible. Many never enter ministry because they do not receive proper training. As a result they are unprepared for the work God has for them. Study and training will bring you confidence as a leader that nothing else will bring.

Bible colleges, seminaries, and church institutes for training leaders are in abundance today. Or, if such training places are not nearby, there are study Bibles, Bible handbooks, Bible commentaries, audio cassette Bible courses, correspondence courses, and teaching videos readily available. But you will need to act.

As Paul wrote to Timothy, "Be diligent to present yourself approved to God, a worker who does not need to be ashamed, rightly dividing the word of truth" (2 Tim. 2:15).

BIBLE PEOPLE WHO LED WITH CONFIDENCE

What comes to your mind when you hear the names of great leaders such as Moses, Joshua, Daniel, and Simon Peter? Somehow, names of leaders in the Bible may evoke unreal images in our minds. Without exception, these were men of great confidence and stamina. But they were very human also. As we study their lives, we discover they had their moments just like everyone else.

Moses

Consider Moses who, though very confident, was at times "beside himself" as he endeavored to lead the rebellious Israelites. What "human reactions" are recorded in the following two instances: (1) Exodus 31:18; 32:19; and (2) Numbers 20:10, 11?

Sometimes Moses wanted to walk away from leadership because Israel murmured against him. At times he even feared for his life, crying out to God that the people were about to stone him (Ex. 17:4). He was truly a confident man, but he had moments when his patience was tested, just as we do.

Yet despite his problems, Moses possessed a confidence that moved him to intercede for rebellious Israel when God was prepared to do away with them. As a result of Moses' intercession, God's anger was turned away (32:9–14). Then, with confidence, Moses stood before Israel and declared the righteous judgments of God (35:1).

With confidence Moses made his way up the mountain where he would die. God was with His servant there on the mountain, and when he died, God took him to be with Himself in heaven (Deut. 34:1–6).

FAITH ALIVE

Where do you experience your greatest frustrations? In the home? On campus? In the workplace?

Describe how you cope with the frustration?

Moses reacted to stress with anger. Write about a situation when you felt like walking away and not coming back, as did Moses.

Joshua

One would hardly expect to see Joshua, Moses' successor, and a man who exemplified confidence, on his face before God in bewilderment. But read Joshua 7:1–10. There he is prostrate before God, not understanding why Israel had just suffered military defeat at Ai, by an army inferior to Israel's (Josh. 7:1–9). What was the problem?

See how, after getting his answer from the Lord, Joshua confidently follows divine directions and deals with the problem. Then what happened? (See vv. 10–26; 8:1–29.) A leader can find solutions to and victory beyond problems as he or she finds confidence and direction by waiting before God.

FAITH ALIVE

Tell of a time when fear gripped your heart as you faced a situation over which you seemed to have no control? How did God make a way of escape and give you victory?

If sin has brought defeat in your life, be assured that if you will deal with it through confession and repentance, God will forgive you. You can then face your situation with confidence and realize victory.

Peter

Peter is so like many of us in his mood swings and behavior. At times he was boldly presumptuous (Matt. 16:22) and at other times fearful (14:30). Sometimes he was self-sacrificing (Mark 1:18) and at other times self-seeking (Matt. 19:27). He was gifted with spiritual insight (John 6:68) yet slow to apprehend the deeper truths (Matt. 15:15, 16). He made two great confessions of his faith in Christ (Matt. 16:16; John 6:69), but he also denied the Lord when He was being tried (Mark 14:67–72).

It was not until Peter was baptized with the Holy Spirit that he emerged as a confident, courageous, and immovable leader and witness for Christ (Acts. 4:19, 20; 5:28, 29, 40, 42).[6] It was then that he truly became the "stone" Jesus said he would be (John 1:42).

    FAITH ALIVE

Describe your personal relationship with the Holy Spirit. Is He personal or impersonal to you? Explain.

John 7:37–39 describes the blessedness of being filled with the Holy Spirit. Those who are filled with the Spirit become channels of spiritual refreshment as they minister with confidence to others. Describe the measure of the fulfillment of these verses in your life.

To what depth and with what force does the Spirit flow from your innermost being? A trickle? A river?

Daniel

The prophet Daniel demonstrated great confidence throughout his life and ministry. Though he experienced severe testing, he seems not to have had the downside we sometimes see in others. His confidence in God's direction for his life was evident at every turn. He would not eat the king's food, lest he become defiled (Dan. 1:8); he would pray when commanded not to (6:7, 10); he would go down into the lion's den if he must, so strong was his confidence in God's providence in his life.

Interestingly, Daniel was victorious in every test. Though he did not *eat* the king's food (1:11–15), what happened?

Though he was thrown into the lion's den as a punishment for praying (6:20–23), what happened? Further, even his enemies were vanquished (6:24). How?

Daniel's triumphs were recorded to inspire us to have a confidence in God as he did. When our rights to pray and to serve God are being threatened, let us go to prayer, confident that God will answer.

THE CONFIDENT:
NOT INTIMIDATED BY THE SUCCESS OF OTHERS

When John the Baptist was told that Jesus and His disciples were baptizing and that great throngs of people were coming to Him, he responded, "A man can receive nothing unless it has been given to him from heaven. . . . He must increase, but I must decrease" (John 3:27, 30). John was secure in his own identity and mission. When he heard of Jesus' success in ministry, he felt no intimidation but rather he rejoiced that he had been called to be the forerunner of the Messiah (vv. 28, 29).

Someone has said that because of His utter confidence in His own identity and mission, Jesus was not at all intimidated by others. When Jesus' disciples were disturbed that those who were not of their number were using His name to exorcise demons, He was not intimidated by the report (Mark 9:39, 49). What was His response?

 ## Faith Alive

Do you ever feel threatened or intimidated by the ministry of another believer? What do you feel is at the root of your feelings, e.g., insecurity, inadequacy, jealousy, envy, etc.)?

What can you learn from John the Baptist's and Jesus' examples?

Confidence: the Results of . . .

Conclude your study on the traits of confidence by reflecting on the major areas considered in this lesson, which are listed in the lefthand column below. Next, rate yourself on each area by putting a check in the appropriate column.

	Very Good	Good	Satisfactory	Needs Improvement
Relationship with God				

	Very Good	Good	Satisfactory	Needs Improvement
Sense of Personal Identity				
Knowing One's Gifting				
Study and Training				
Not Intimidated by Others' Success				

Where do you stand regarding confidence? What areas need strengthening? Pray that your own confidence may be strengthened in these areas. If you are participating in a group study, pray for others in the group who may be facing some real challenges to their confidence.

1. James Strong, *The New Strong's Exhaustive Concordance of the Bible; Greek Dictionary of the New Testament* (Nashville, TN: Thomas Nelson, 1990), #3954.

2. Jerry Cook, "Stress" (Arroyo Grande, CA: Speaker, Pastor's Conference, Southern California District of Foursquare Churches, Oct. 13, 1993).

3. Leighton Ford, *Transforming Leadership* (Downer's Grove, IL: InterVarsity Press, 1991), 37–38.

4. *Spirit-Filled Life Bible* (Nashville, TN: Thomas Nelson Publishers, 1991), 1600, "Kingdom Dynamics: John 13:1–7, Secure."

5. Ibid., 1587, note on John 7:15.

6. *The New Chain-Reference Bible, Third Improved Edition*, Frank Charles Thompson, Ed. and Comp. (Indianapolis, IN: B. B. Kirkbride Bible Co., 1934), 106, "Peter, 2746."

Lesson 6/ Encouraging Faith in Others

Faith may be encouraged in several ways—for example, through the teaching and preaching of the Word, the manifestation of the gifts of the Spirit, seeing men and women come to Christ, or hearing reports of victory through the testimony of fellow believers. All these various ways encourage us to believe God for His continued blessings for others, and in our own lives as well.

Perhaps one of the strongest means of encouraging faith is to hear the testimonies of those who have had answers to prayer, or who have received a healing, a miracle, or a deliverance from some bondage in their lives. To hear of a family member who has finally come to Christ after years of prayer encourages us to believe for the conversion of our own family members as well.

Leaders may encourage faith in the hearts of those they lead by sharing testimonies of victory they have experienced. This requires courage and vulnerability on the leaders' part. Some may hesitate to share because of the danger of shattering the image of invincibility some people hold of spiritual leaders. But when it is done with wisdom and discretion, it can prove to be fruitful. People who are being led will bond with leaders who are honest about their own struggles and subsequent victories.

A young pastor and his wife set out to plant a church in a Boston suburb. They worked hard and long to gather enough people to start a church. He did manual labor part-time to provide for his family of four.

One day the wife said, "It's dinnertime and we have no food and no money." The young pastor said to his wife, "Go ahead and set the table. God will provide the food we need." While the table was being set, the doorbell rang. When they opened the door, there stood several people on the porch holding bags of groceries for the pastor and his family.

Where did this young pastor get the faith to say what he said regarding divine provision? He got it from reading the testimony of a senior pastor who experienced the identical need years before, and God miraculously supplied for him. This senior pastor had experienced seventy years of miracles from the hand of God.

HEROES OF FAITH

The Holy Spirit saw the value of testimonies of faith when He inspired the writer of Hebrews to include an entire chapter devoted to them. After commencing chapter 11 with a description of faith (vv. 1–3), the author then proceeds to bring before us a retinue of past heroes of faith (vv. 4–40).

The following exercise will help you learn about the heroes listed in faith's "Hall of Fame" in Hebrews 11. Look up the verses listed in column 1, and then write down the hero's or group's name in column 2. In column 3, note the experience of faith whereby each gained recognition.

Heroes of Faith
(Hebrews 11)

	Hero	Experience of Faith
v. 4		
v. 5		
v. 7		
vv. 8–10, 17–19		
v. 11		
v. 20		

Heroes of Faith
(Hebrews 11)

	Hero	Experience of Faith
v. 21		
v. 22		
v. 23		
vv. 24–28		
v. 29		

 FAITH ALIVE

Choose one of the preceding heroes of faith and write down how your own faith is particularly encouraged by that person or group.

FAITH'S ULTIMATE CONFESSION

"This chapter [Heb. 11] records glorious victories of faith's champions, yet vv. 13–16 speak of those who died, 'not having received the promises.' Even then, the Bible says 'these all died in the faith,' being content to confess that they were only strangers and pilgrims traveling, as it were, through the land: 'For true believers, to live by faith is to die by faith' (Wycliffe).

"The key to the 'confession' (v. 13) of this admirable group in Heb. 11 is that when given a promise by God, as were Abraham and his descendants, they became 'fully persuaded' that the promise was true. Thus they embraced (literally 'greeted') that promise in their hearts. The word 'confess' helps us to understand how easily these of the gallery of faith established their ways before God and left the testimony, which His Word records with tribute. While each of these persons did receive *many* victories through faith, the text says that none of them received *everything* that was promised. Whether or not we receive what we 'confess' (ask, pray, or hope for) does not change the behavior or the attitude of the steadfast believer. Faith's worship and walk do not depend on answered or unanswered prayers. Our confession of His lordship in our lives is to be consistent—a daily celebration, with deep gratitude. (Heb. 4:11–13/Rev. 12:11)"[1]

Those who died possessed a heavenly hope. We, as they did, live by faith in this world, but our faith looks forward to the time when all the promises God has made to the righteous will be fulfilled.

  WORD WEALTH

The best description of faith is found in Hebrews 11:1, "Now faith is the substance of things hoped for, the evidence of things not seen."
1. **Faith,** *pistis,* means: assurance, or firm conviction.
2. **Substance,** *elpidzomenon* (el-pi-dzo-*men*on), means: to hope, to expect, or to have hope and confidence in, trust.

FAITH TO POSSESS THE LAND

Although Joshua's name is not mentioned in the above list, he too was a man of faith and sought to encourage faith in others. When the twelve Hebrew men returned from spying out the land of Canaan, it was only two of the spies, Joshua and Caleb, who tried to encourage faith in the others. They believed that God would give Israel the land in spite of the obstacles that stood in the way. The other ten would not receive the encouragement to believe, and they died in the wilderness. But Joshua and Caleb's faith endured, and they lived to enter the land and to take possession of it.

Joshua had many experiences in his early life as a soldier and aid to Moses that contributed to his faith.

Some of his faith-building experiences are recorded in the following passages. Read each one and record how you think the events served to build Joshua's faith in God.

Exodus 17:8–15—Leading the battle against Amalek

Exodus 24:12, 17—Accompanying Moses partway up Mount Sinai

Exodus 33:7–11—Accompanying Moses to the tabernacle of meeting

 FAITH ALIVE

What have you experienced that has helped to build your faith? List these events and note how your faith has been strengthened.

DEALING WITH NEGATIVE POPULAR OPINION

Joshua was finally faced with hard choices, and most of the decisions he made went against popular opinion. He wanted the people to focus on God's promises rather than on their negative circumstances. Read Numbers 13 and 14:1–30, and answer the following questions.

What were the spies supposed to look for? (13:17–20)

What did the spies find? (vv. 23–29)

What made the difference in the way Joshua and Caleb saw the land compared to the way the other ten spies saw the land? (vv. 30–33; 14:6–8)

How would you describe the prevailing mood of the people after they heard the report of the twelve? (14:1–10)

What does their attitude tell you about their faith?

The people requested that the spies be sent into Canaan (Deut. 1:19–24) because they would not believe God's word (v. 20). Instead they chose to rely on human wisdom (that spies first be sent). It was not enough that God would go before them; they wanted human representatives as well.

When Joshua and Caleb came back with a positive report based on their faith in the power of God, they were willing to do the unpopular thing, which was to call the people to trust in God.

> The leader does not condition his appeal to the sentiment or mood of the times. Spiritual advance requires faith, and unbelief will never see beyond the difficulties. Unbelief sees "walled cities" and "giants" rather than the presence and power of God."[2]

FAITH IN ACTION

Responses were not always negative when Joshua sought to encourage faith in the hearts of the people. As he obeyed God's voice and put his faith into action in leading Israel, they often responded. In the following passages, how did faith increase greatly in the people's hearts as they saw faith in action in their leader Joshua? (Read also James 2:17.)

Joshua 3:1, 9–17—A river to cross

Joshua 6:2–5, 12–21—A walled city to conquer

Joshua 10:1–27 (note v. 25)—Threatened by confederate kings

 FAITH ALIVE

The conquests of Joshua and the Israelites over their enemies in the Promised Land may be seen as symbolic of the spiritual warfare experienced in the Christian life, e.g., believers reclaiming spiritual ground lost as a result of the Fall. Paul describes that warfare with these words:

For we do not wrestle against flesh and blood, but against principalities, against powers, against the rulers of the darkness of this age, against spiritual hosts of wickedness in the heavenly places (Eph. 6:12).

As Joshua's victories were won by faith, so too are the victories won by Christians today (see I John 5:4).

Who does Ephesians 6:12 say is our true enemy?

List people, circumstances, or situations in your life that are sources of conflict or challenge to you.

Reflect on whom/what you listed and jot down the true source of your problems and challenges.

What does 1 John 5:4 say is our victory? To whom does it belong?

Perhaps one of the most stirring and challenging demonstrations of Joshua's faith and his ability to encourage faith in the hearts of his followers is to be found in Joshua 24:14–22. Joshua's leadership of Israel was about to come to an end, and his greatest concern for the people before he stepped down was that their faith be in God and not in idols.

Read Joshua 24:14–22 and discover the approach used by this great leader in stirring the people to make a declaration of their faith in God.

 PROBING THE DEPTHS

A study of religion in the Old Testament reveals a tension between Israel's true spiritual conception of God, their worship due to Him (distinctions of their faith) and the pressure of idolatry. Idolatry, when embraced by the people, resulted in the perversion and materialization of their religious experience. In other words, it deteriorated their faith.[3]

In what way is the tendency of Israel to engage in idolatry revealed in Joshua 24:14, 15, 23?

How does Joshua declare his position of faith in God before the people? (Josh. 24:15)

How were the people affected by Joshua's bold declaration of faith and obedience to God? (vv. 16–18, 21, 22, 24)

FAITH ALIVE

Joshua commanded the people to "put away the foreign gods" (Josh. 24:23). As God's people today, we are not without the temptation to make gods of people or things and put our faith in them rather than in the true and only Lord.

List the "gods" that Christians might be tempted to put their trust in today (e.g., money, power, pleasures).

Has a "god" won your trust? If so how do you plan to "put away" this god?

A PARTICULAR KIND OF FAITH

Faith can be used in a general sense. For example, I might say, "I have faith in that person without doubt or question." One might also have faith in something that cannot be proved. But the faith we are considering in this lesson is a specific kind of faith. It is faith that has a source; it is essential in order to be saved; it is essential in the believer's life; it has been tested and proved; it has great power.

The Bible is clear with regard to the **source of faith.** To try to find it elsewhere is an exercise in futility. To try to produce it in and of oneself is an impossibility. In the following verses you will discover the source of faith. Write in the source you discover in each verse, and then write out the verse in full. Take time to commit the verse to memory.

Romans 10:17

> Source:

> Verse:

According to Romans 10:17, what must we do to receive faith through this source?

1 Corinthians 12:9

> Source:

> Verse:

How will faith come to us through this source?

Galatians 5:22
Note: "Faithfulness" in this verse (NKJV) is translated "faith" in some other versions.

> Source:

> Verse:

What can we do to assure that faith in this form will be present in our lives?

Faith is essential in the believer's life for several reasons. For each of the following verses, write out the portion that supports the "It . . ." statement.

It assures success (2 Chron. 20:20)

It is a defensive weapon (Eph. 6:16)

It is a requirement for pleasing God (Heb. 11:6)

It is to be exercised in prayer (James 1:5, 6)

It is what the Christian lives by (Hab. 2:4b)

It will move mountains (Matt. 21:21b)

Our faith will be tested, but we have the assurance that God places certain limitations on testing.

> No temptation has overtaken you except such as is common to man; but God is faithful, who will not allow you to be tempted beyond what you are able, but with the temptation will also make the way of escape, that you may be able to bear it (1 Cor. 10:13).

STRENGTHENING OUR FAITH

We find out just how strong our faith is when we undergo tests or trials. That we are followers of Christ doesn't exempt us from difficulties.

Jesus' disciples did not always have strong faith even though they had the visible presence of Christ with them. It was not as if they had to send a prayer heavenward and wait for an answer. The Answer was right there with them, and still they struggled from time to time because of their weak faith.

Verses in Matthew 6:25–34 describe instances of weak faith on the part of the disciples.

With what were they preoccupied in their thoughts?

How did Jesus proceed to strengthen their faith?

 FAITH ALIVE

From time to time many of us become preoccupied with temporal needs. The uncertainty of employment seems to threaten the stability of our finances. Prices are going higher, but salaries remain the same. Fringe benefits that used to be there may be gone. It is a test of faith.

Reviewing Matthew 6:25–34 may strengthen our faith. We are higher than the birds and the lilies in the order of creation. If God takes care of the lesser of His creation, surely He will take care of us. God has promised to meet every need.

What is it that worries you most?

What do Jesus' words, "Do not worry about your life," mean to you?

What does "seek first the kingdom of God and His righteousness" mean to you?

If you had one wish, which one of the following list would you choose?

__Win the Clearinghouse Sweepstakes

__ Have a home all paid for

__Be healthy the rest of my life

__Be successful in my career

__Be well thought of and acceptable by others

__Have an intimate personal relationship with the heavenly Father who cares for me

What will you do to counteract worry so that you might focus on advancing God's kingdom?

One day as a pastor was leaving a supermarket, he could hardly believe what the bill totalled. He thought, "How can I afford to feed my family on my salary?" Then God spoke to his heart, "Son, if the groceries get to be twice the amount you just paid, the money will be there to buy them. I will see to that." Our Father is faithful, fully able to give us our "daily bread."

Read Matthew 8:23–27 and answer the following questions.

What was troubling the disciples on this occasion?

What did Jesus say about their faith?

How did He encourage their faith?

Read Matthew 14:22–32 and answer the following questions.

Which disciple responded in faith?

What do you think of the request he made of the Lord? Was it presumptuous?

What caused his faith to falter?

How was the disciples' faith strengthened from this experience?

   FAITH ALIVE

God is patient with us when we ask for things that are impractical or foolish. Peter's faith was strong when he asked the Lord to call him to come to Him on the water. But as he got out of the boat and began his walk toward Jesus, his faith weakened when he saw the turbulence of the water. God may even let us get in over our heads because of the things we ask for in faith. But He will not forsake us. He will extend His hand and lift us up. We learn as we go along just what kind of things we should ask for when we pray.

The Lord is good,
A stronghold in the day of trouble;
And He knows those who trust in Him.

Nahum 1:7

1. *Spirit-Filled Life Bible* (Nashville, TN: Thomas Nelson Publishers, 1991), 1885–1886, "Kingdom Dynamics: Heb. 11:13–16, Faith's Confession is Steadfast."

2. Ibid., 212, "Kingdom Dynamics: Num. 13:1—14:45; Josh. 6:1–27; 10:1–43, Resisting Popular Opinion."

3. For additional information regarding idolatry as it is dealt with in the Old and New Testaments and the negative effect it had on God's people, consult *Nelson's Illustrated Bible Dictionary* (Nashville: Thomas Nelson Publishers, 1986).

Lesson 7/Leadership God's Way

One of the most repeated prayers we hear is, "Lord, lead, guide, and direct, that we may go in the way You would have us to go." Do you ever wonder if there is really a difference between God leading, God guiding, and God directing?

The dictionary shows "lead" to mean "position at the front." So, to ask God to lead us is to ask that He take the front position, and wherever He leads, we will follow. "Guide" means very much the same as "lead." But interestingly, "direct" means "to regulate the activities or course of a person or group." In the theater, the director is the one who supervises the production of a show. He is usually responsible for action, lighting, music, and rehearsals. Just as the show is totally dependent on the director, our lives are like that with God. We can't go on without the direction of the One who wrote the script and who has a part for each of us to play. So we ask Him to "direct" us.

The reason we use such prayer is that it expresses the intense desire of our hearts to be led in God's way and not in our own. We don't want to go astray. As an expression of our dependence upon Him we ask God to lead, guide, and direct not only our activities but even our thoughts.

Many of our Christian hymns express the desire for or the acknowledgement of God's leadership in our lives: "God Leads Us Along"; "Guide Me, O Thou Great Jehovah"; "He Leadeth Me"; "If Jesus Goes with Me"; "It Is Glory Just to Walk with Him"; "O Master, Let Me Walk with Thee"; and "Savior, Like a Shepherd Lead Us."

Consider the words of just one of these.

God Leads Us Along

In shady green pastures, so rich and so sweet,
God leads His dear children along;
Where the water's cool flow bathes the weary one's feet,
God leads His dear children along.

Sometimes on the mount where the sun shines so bright,
God leads His dear children along;
Sometimes in the valley in darkest of night,
God leads His dear children along.

Though sorrows befall us, and Satan oppose,
God leads His dear children along;
Through grace we can conquer, defeat all our foes,
God leads His dear children along.

Chorus
Some through the waters, some through the flood,
Some through the fire, but all through the blood;
Some through great sorrow, but God gives a song;
In the night season and all the day long.[1]

—G. A. Young

The writer speaks of a variety of experiences, describing how God is leading in all of them. His presence and power sanctifies each experience so that all things work together for our good and for God's glory (Rom. 8:28).

Write the lyrics of a song that means much to you and that describes God's leading/keeping/providing hand.

GOD'S WAY OF LEADING IN THE OLD TESTAMENT

The following Old Testament passages provide insight as to how the Lord led Israel and, in some instances, led individuals.

Read and reflect upon the following passages. Then write briefly of how the Lord led in each instance.

Genesis 24:1–27

Exodus 13:17, 18

Deuteronomy 31:30—32:7, 9–12

Psalm 23:2, 3

Psalm 107:1–7

Isaiah 63:7, 10–14

As we read through the Old Testament, we learn that God led Israel with power, with compassion, with tenderness, even taking "them [Israel] by the hand" (Jer. 31:32). The psalmist speaks of being led by the Lord "into paths of righteousness" and "by the still waters." God leads His people not from a distance but is present and involved in their lives daily. God loved, cared for, and led His people Israel through leaders whom He appointed over them.

All of the appointed leaders had to learn to lead God's way and, with few exceptions, they were slow learners. Some tried to lead by human reason, without seeking God's way; and, as a result, failed in their efforts. Some tried to lead by fleshly might, not relying on God's power, and they suffered great loss. Some tried to substitute their own plans for God's plans, only to end up frustrated. But those who had a heart for God emerged as outstanding leaders.

GIDEON LED GOD'S WAY

Gideon is a good example of someone who led God's people in God's way. In Gideon's day, because Israel had forsaken God, they were overrun by their enemies, the Midianites, who terrorized them, robbed them of their harvest, and left the land desolate. This made life intolerable for the people (Judg. 6:1–5), but in the midst of their distress, "the children of Israel cried out to the Lord" (v. 6). As a result, God answered their cry and called Gideon to deliver them from the tyranny of the Midianites, and he proved to be a leader who led God's way. In Judges 6—8 you can trace the steps of Gideon's leadership, from the time of his call to his subduing of the Midianites.

Describe the remarkable way in which God summoned Gideon to leadership (Judg. 6:11, 12, 14).

How did God assure Gideon of success? (vv. 16–23)

What was the first thing Gideon did at the command of God after his call to leadership? (vv. 24–28)

How was his faith severely tested before going into battle with the Midianites? (7:2–8)

Why did God reduce Israel's army? (v. 2)

What was the war cry of the 300 soldiers as they approached the enemy? What is the significance of the wording of the war cry? (v. 20)

What were the rewards of Gideon's leadership for doing things God's way? (7:19–8:21, 28)

 ### FAITH ALIVE

God reduced Gideon's army from 32,000 soldiers down to 300. He was not encouraging risk-taking, He was building trust. God is able to save by many or by few, and in this case He chose few. This runs counter to our success-oriented culture that believes bigger is better.

Note a time in your life when God led you to do something, the accomplishment of which required complete trust in Him. You obeyed, and the outcome was even beyond your expectations. Describe the effect the experience had upon your relationship with God and on your faith.

ABIMELECH RESISTED GOD'S WAY

Although Gideon proved to be a leader who led God's way, his son Abimelech did not follow in his footsteps. Whereas Gideon refused when the people of Israel asked him to rule over them (Judg. 8:22, 23), Abimelech, his son, had a lust for power and wanted to be king. After his father's death, Abimelech immediately took steps to gain rulership over Israel. Judges 9:1–6 reveals Abimelech's conspiracy. Describe what he did.

The reading of Judges 9:7–21 reveals the courage it took for Jotham to stand up to his brother Abimelech. Jotham was enraged at the injustice done to his father's house and was ready to speak out against it. He presented himself before Abimelech and the men of Shechem at the risk of losing his life, and in prophetic parabolic language he declared the wickedness of Abimelech and told of his downfall that was forthcoming. Relate the message Jotham declared.

FAITH ALIVE

Record a time in your life when you had to speak out against unfairness or wrong, perhaps even at the risk of retaliation. What was the issue? Where did you get the motivation to speak out? What was the outcome?

GOD'S WAY OF LEADING IN THE NEW TESTAMENT

God's way of leading His people changes when we come to the New Testament. Whereas He led through the patriarchs, prophets, judges, and kings in the Old Testament, in the New He leads through a variety of gifts and ministry offices that He has placed in the church. (Although the gifts of the Spirit have been considered in Lesson 5, you will view them from a different perspective in this lesson.)

Some see the gifts of the Holy Spirit as being given to the church by each member of the Trinity. Gifts that are listed in Romans 12:6–8 are seen as being given by the Father (basic life purpose and motivation); those in Ephesians 4:11, as being given by the Son (to equip and facilitate the church body); and those in 1 Corinthians 12:8–10, the *charismata*, as being given by the Holy Spirit.

In the space provided below, list the gifts placed in each of these suggested categories.

Gifts of the Father Rom. 12:6–8	Gifts of the Son Eph. 4:11	Gifts of the Spirit 1 Cor. 12:8–10

Every believer has been gifted in some way (Eph. 4:7) so as to be able to participate in ministry to the body of Christ. The abundance of gifts to the church reflects the love and care that God has for each of us. He cares for us and leads us through His

Word, His Spirit, and through the gifts He has given to the church. It is His will that each believer enjoy the fullness of the Spirit, grow to full stature in Christ, and be equipped to minister.

PASTOR-CENTERED CHURCH

Leading God's way means different things to different people. There are differences of opinion as to the way leadership is to be implemented in the church and also with regard to the role of the laity in leadership.

While some hold to a pastor-centered institutional leadership model, others see the pastor as a "player coach," e.g., one who disciples and equips others for ministry while he is involved in ministry alongside them.

Some see the sheep (congregation) as dependent upon the shepherd (pastor). The shepherd leads, waters, pastures, and protects the flock. He does everything for them, so they become dependent upon him. As a result, there is little opportunity for the sheep to develop their own leadership gifts. If they lead at all, it is usually in the "nonspiritual" areas of church life.

EVERY BELIEVER IS A PRIEST

There are those who, though they recognize the role of and need for pastors, hold to the teaching that every member of Christ's body is a priest before God and to one another. This view decentralizes the focus of spiritual leadership. It sees Christ's ministry gifts to the church—apostles, prophets, evangelists, pastors, and teachers (Eph. 4:11)—as equipping in nature. These leaders are Jesus' gifts to the church, to equip members of the church so that *they* may do the work of the ministry.

The every-believer-a-priest view encourages all believers to prayerfully ascertain what gifts they possess and to function in ministry accordingly. To assist them, spiritual profile tests and spiritual gifts inventories may be administered. In addition, training seminars are provided on how the gifts function.

Those who hold this view of church ministry testify to growth that takes place in the individual believer's life, as well as the dynamic spiritual relationships that develop within the body and an increase in the number of new believers added to the church.

 FAITH ALIVE

What are the spiritual gifts that function in your personal ministry?

How did you become aware of those gifts being present in your life and ministry?

How would you describe your church's ministry model? Pastor-centered? People-centered? Other?

What are the advantages of the ministry model used in your church?

What are the disadvantages, if any?

WHAT GOD'S LEADING IS NOT

True spiritual leadership is not by false charisma, that is, not by human magnetism or genius. Personal charm may get a leader a following for a while, but charm alone can wear thin quickly if not accompanied by substantive ministry that feeds the soul and gives direction for life. The Greeks came to the disciples and said, "We would see Jesus" (John 12:20, 21). People of discernment hunger for Jesus and need leaders who can so minister to them, not charm or manipulate them.

The leaders of the seven churches of Asia, whom Jesus addressed in letters recorded in Revelation 2 and 3, are referred to as "stars" (1:20). They are portrayed as stars being held in Jesus' right hand (v. 16). Bible commentator Matthew Henry writes, "He had in his right hand seven stars, that is, the ministers of the seven churches, who are under his direction, have all their light and influence from him, and are secured and preserved by him."[2]

What a blessed condition: not our light and influence but His, not our holding power but His. Not our direction but His, not our charm but His anointing and calling that is leading God's way!

John the Baptist was a great prophet. Multitudes of people came to hear his call to repentance and to be baptized by him. When some began to wonder if he was the Christ, he made it quite clear to them that he was not. John's Gospel records John the Baptist's response to the people. Read John 3:28–30 and record your responses to the following questions.

How did John the Baptist identify himself?

What allegory did he use to describe his own emotions?

What did he say that asserted the supremacy of Jesus?

What does this tell us about John the Baptist?

John the Baptist had it right, and we too must get it right. Jesus is to increase through our ministries and we must decrease. He alone is the Chief Cornerstone, the only sure foundation. Let us lead people not by our charm but to the Rock upon which they may build their lives securely.

FAITH ALIVE

How do you express the role and place of Christ in your life?

How can you lead others so as to direct their attention and their loyalties to Christ alone and not to human leadership?

TAKING CONTROL?

Jesus' disciples were familiar with two leadership styles, both of which exercised negative control over the people. Those models were demonstrated 1) through the way the Gentiles were lorded over by their great men, and 2) by the way the Jewish religious leaders (Pharisees) exercised control over their people.

What did Jesus say with regard to such Gentile leaders? (Matt. 20:25). What was His answer regarding us, as His disciples who exercise leadership?(Matt. 20:26)

The Jewish religious leaders of Christ's time were supposed to be models whom the people could follow. In fact, they were quite the opposite of what they were supposed to be. They were the "Pharisees," which means "the separated ones."

This immediately tells you something of the way they perceived themselves—apart from and above all others. Instead, what did Jesus call them, and why? (Matt. 15:7; 23:3)

Jesus saw them as prideful and pious, "But all their works they do to be seen by men. They make their phylacteries broad and enlarge the borders of their garments" (Matt. 23:5). Jesus also noted their lust for the place of honor. "They love the best places at feasts, the best seats in the synagogues" (v. 6). This is not the style of leadership Jesus would have His disciples pattern their lives after. He said, "But he who is greatest among you shall be your servant" (v. 11).

BEHIND THE SCENES

Phylacteries were small scrolls of paper on which were written these four paragraphs of the law: Exodus 13:2–11; 13:11–16; Deuteronomy 6:4–9; 11:13–21. These were sown up in leather and were worn on their foreheads and left arms. It was a tradition of the elders and was done in literal obedience to Deuteronomy 6:8 and Proverbs 7:3. The Jewish religious community took these references literally.

God also instructed the Jews to make borders or fringes upon their garments (Num. 15:38), to distinguish them from other nations and to remind them that they were His peculiar people. But the Pharisees made their borders large, so that people would take notice of them, to make them appear to be more religious than others. They prided themselves by affecting superiority and preeminence.

A servant does not seek to control, but seeks opportunities to serve others. Jesus perfectly modeled this servant spirit before His disciples. He ministered to the poor, the hungry, the disenfranchised, the sick, the widows. He stooped to wash His disciples' feet, taking the place of a servant. Jesus was not seeking control of people; He spent time setting them free! (Matt. 20:28).

TEAMWORK

One person cannot be all things to all people. We all have blind spots. Teamwork is needed if adequate leadership is to be provided. Jesus and His disciples worked as a team. He taught them and trained them, and when He left earth to return to heaven He was able to leave His work in their hands.

Where there is personality-centered leadership there is weak structure, but where there is team leadership the church structure will be strengthened. The apostle Paul said, "For we are labourers together with God" (1 Cor. 3:9, KJV. Read also Phil. 1:27; Col. 2:2). If teamwork is to exist, then there can be no loners or "Lone Rangers."

 ## FAITH ALIVE

Here are some tips for those who desire to lead God's way.

- Develop an intimate relationship and walk with God.
- Live a life focused on doing the thing God has called you to do, and do it God's way. Be led by the Holy Spirit. Let Him set the agenda. Live a disciplined life so as to yield maximum fruitage.
- Pray about the type of ministry God would have you develop. Will it be a leader-centered or every-believer-a-priest ministry? In either case, seek to enable each believer you lead to reach his or her full potential of growth and ministry in Christ.
- Be an emissary of love to a world that is hurting.
- Let it be known that your sufficiency is not of yourself but of God. The miracles you have experienced and the achievement of things thought impossible all point to the One who gave the grace and who released His power to bring it all about.
- Be one through whom the Spirit of God can speak a fresh word to the church. Preach and teach the Word with the anointing of the Spirit and be a vessel ready to speak the extemporaneous word of prophecy when it is the will of the Spirit to do so.
- Be rich in the knowledge of the Bible.

1. "God Leads Us Along," *Songs of Praise* (Springfield, MO: Gospel Publishing House, 1935), 284.

2. Matthew Henry, *Matthew Henry's Commentary on the Whole Bible, Vol. VI* (New York: Fleming H. Revell Company), 1122.

Lesson 8/Reliance on the Anointing

When one is yielded to God and relies on the anointing of the Spirit wonderful things take place! There is progressive, personal sanctification that is manifested in the fruit of the Spirit. "But the fruit of the Spirit is love, joy, peace, longsuffering, kindness, goodness, faithfulness, gentleness, self-control. Against such there is no law" (Gal. 5:22, 23). There is the teaching of spiritual truths that can come only by the guidance and illumination of the Spirit (John 16:12–14). The deep things of God can only be known by those who rely upon the teaching ministry of the Spirit (1 Cor. 2:9, 10). The Spirit enables the believer to apply the truths of the Word of God to his or her particular situation. The Spirit also enables the believer to properly worship and love God (John 4:24).

In addition to all of the personal blessings derived from reliance upon the anointing of the Spirit, there are the blessings of the Spirit's anointing in ministry to the body of Christ. The natural and spiritual gifts one possesses for ministry are dependent upon the power of the Spirit if they are to be exercised effectively. Jesus likened the anointing of the Spirit to rivers of living water flowing from within the believer (7:38). Rivers of living water speaks of divine energy, energy that enables the believer to serve God effectively. One may possess great spiritual gifts and yet not be used of God if there is not a reliance upon His anointing. On the other hand, one may have few gifts and yet be greatly used of God because of a reliance upon the anointing.

"Anoint," according to Webster's dictionary, means "to apply oil to as a sacred rite especially for consecration; to choose by or as if by divine election."[1]

WORD WEALTH

Anointed, *mashach* (mah–*shahch*), means to anoint, to rub with oil, especially in order to consecrate someone or something. Appearing almost 70 times, *mashach* refers to the custom of rubbing or smearing with sacred oil to consecrate holy persons or holy things. . . . The most important derivative of *mashach* is *mashiyach* (Messiah), "anointed one." As Jesus was and is the promised Anointed One, His title came to be "Jesus the Messiah." Messiah was translated into Greek as *Christos,* thus His designation, "Jesus Christ."[2]

ANOINTING IN THE OLD TESTAMENT

Articles and persons were anointed in the Old Testament to signify holiness, or separation unto God.

Read the following references and then write in after each reference the articles that received the anointing.

Genesis 28:18

Exodus 30:25–29

Isaiah 21:5

Enter after the references below the names of the persons who were set apart by anointing.

Leviticus 8:30

1 Samuel 16:12, 13

1 Kings 1:39

Anointing in the Old Testament could also signify appointment to a special office or function in the purposes of God. In the story of Abraham and Sarah before King Abimelech of Gerar (Gen. 20:1–7), we see that God considered Abraham to be an anointed prophet. Even more importantly, Abraham had a special place in God's redemptive plan. He was to be a forebearer of the Christ. And even though King Abimelech could have punished Abraham for lying to him, God intervened and rebuked the king for Abraham's sake. God's word of rebuke to the king is recorded by the psalmist, "Do not touch My anointed ones, and do My prophets no harm" (Ps. 105:15). Later, David would not kill Saul because he had been anointed of God (1 Sam. 24:6, 7).

Anointing in the Old Testament also symbolized special enduement for ministry to God. Only those uniquely called of God received the Holy Spirit. By contrast, under the New Covenant every believer is offered the Promise of the Father (Joel 2:28; Luke 24:49), the active presence of the Holy Spirit. From the following verses, make note of the *special equipping* associated with the Spirit's outpouring upon the individuals for a present or future ministry.

Exodus 28:41

1 Samuel 9:26–10:9

1 Samuel l 16:11–13

1 Kings 1:34, 35; 1 Chronicles 9:22, 25

Isaiah 61:1–3

To the Jewish mind, or to anyone familiar with Old Testament practice, an anointing represented a divine dedication and a consecration to a holy office.

Basically, the anointing was an act of God, as is seen in the anointing of Saul as king over Israel. After Samuel had taken a flask of oil and poured it on Saul's head he said, "Is it not because *the Lord* [emphasis added] has anointed you commander over His inheritance?" (1 Sam. 10:1).

CONTRASTS AND SIMILARITIES

One cannot help but observe the stark contrast between Saul and David, the first and second kings of Israel. Although both had received the anointing of the Holy Spirit to be king of Israel, their lives were opposite in character and destiny.

Because of Saul's disobedience, God rejected him from reigning over Israel (1 Sam. 16:1). Following his rejection by God, it is said that "the Spirit of the Lord departed from Saul, and a distressing spirit from the Lord troubled him" (v. 14). About this, A. B. Simpson wrote:

> Here [1 Sam. 10] we see the Spirit coming upon a man almost unsought, and apparently without any spiritual preparation. It was the Spirit of God coming for service, giving him power to prophesy, to conquer, to rule, the enduement for service rather than for personal experience.
>
> There is a real danger just at this point. It is a very serious thing to want the Holy Ghost simply to give us power to work for God. It is much more important that we should receive the Holy Spirit for personal character and personal holiness. Perhaps the deep secret of Saul's failure was that, like Balaam, he had power to witness and to work rather than to live and obey.[3]

In the verse preceding that which tells about the departure of the Holy Spirit from Saul, we read, "Then Samuel took the horn of oil and anointed him [David] in the midst of his brothers; and the Spirit of the Lord came upon David from that day forward" (1 Sam. 16:13). But David was not anointed for power only; he was also anointed for wisdom and grace. David, as a young man, had already experienced the presence of the Lord in his life (17:34–36). His anointing for rulership was but an extension of what he had already lived out in relationship. He conducted himself in such a manner that he gained the respect of his master Saul (vv. 19–22) and others with whom he came in contact. Throughout David's life the power and the anointing of the Spirit was evident.

FAITH ALIVE

David and Saul behaved quite differently. Take time to read the following passages to discover their behavioral differences, and then answer the following questions.

Saul: 1 Samuel 13:1–15; 14:24–46; 15:1–23; 18:6–13; 19:1–24; 22:6–19; 24; 28:1–20.

David: 1 Samuel 17; 18:13–16; 23:1–4; 24:1–7; 26:1–11.

How did each respond to the anointing?

What was the relationship of each to the Lord?

How did God view each of them?

What might we learn from studying their lives?

When Elijah came to the end of his prophetic ministry, God told him to anoint Elisha to be his successor.

And Elisha the son of Shaphat of Abel Meholah you shall anoint as prophet in your [Elijah's] place. . . . So he departed from there, and found Elisha the son of Shaphat, who was plowing with twelve yoke of oxen before him, and he was with the twelfth. Then Elijah passed by him and threw his mantel on him (1 Kin. 19:16, 19).

"That Elijah threw his mantel on him symbolized that he was electing Elisha to receive the authority and power of his office (see v. 16)."[4] That the authority, power, and anointing did come upon Elisha is evident in the ministry God gave him after Elijah was taken away.

There were many similarities in the ministries of Elijah and Elisha. Both had been anointed by the Spirit, and by relying on the Spirit's anointing they were able to do mighty works.

Discover the similarities in the anointed ministries of Elijah and Elisha by researching the passages below and noting the "similarities" in the right hand column.

Elijah	Elisha	Similarities
2 Kin. 2:8	2 Kin. 2:14	
1 Kin. 18:41–45	2 Kin. 3:9–20	
1 Kin. 17:17–24	2 Kin. 4:18–37	
1 Kin. 21:19–22	2 Kin. 8:7–10	
2 Kin. 1:9–12	2 Kin. 2:23–25	

Elijah had been Elisha's mentor and role model, but Elisha desired something more. He wanted a double portion of the Spirit that had been upon Elijah. He saw great needs that had to be met among the people, and he knew that great needs could only be met by great power. He went on to function in full reliance upon the Holy Spirit's power and, as a result, God was able to use him mightily.

 FAITH ALIVE

Mentoring and discipling are two important aspects of leadership training. We see this demonstrated between Elijah and Elisha. At some point in the discipling process, the disciple comes of age and begins to function in the ministry God has given him or her. In a sense, the mantel is handed down. There comes an anointing for ministry as the disciple reaches maturity in the Lord.

Record where you are in the leadership training process, e.g., are you a mentor, a disciple? Have you had the
mantel of leadership passed on to you? Are you satisfied with
where you are in the process? What are your aspirations for
ministry?

Chapter 2 of 2 Kings reveals a great deal about Elisha's zeal
to be an anointed leader. He was insistent upon being with his
master, Elijah, right up to his being taken into heaven. When
Elijah told him not to accompany him any further, Elisha's
response was one of determination, "As the Lord lives, and as
your soul lives, I will not leave you" (v. 2). He persistently followed until Elijah was gone, and then he got the double portion
he desired.

The Old Testament reveals that the anointing was the official sign that the priests, kings, and prophets were chosen and
dedicated to their respective offices. It also reveals the importance of reliance upon the anointing of the Holy Spirit for effective ministry to God. David's life in particular points up the
value of reliance upon the Holy Spirit to work holiness in one's
life as well as anointing for ministry.

ANOINTING IN THE NEW TESTAMENT

While the Old Testament shows that the Holy Spirit was
given to certain and few individuals to equip them for special
service, in the New Testament, the promise was that the Holy
Spirit will be poured out upon all flesh. Men and women, young
and old, people of all nations would experience the anointing of
the Spirit, or "the promise" of Holy Spirit enablement for life,
ministry and service.

In the account of the birth of Christ, Luke tells us that His
conception was by the Holy Spirit. "And the angel answered
and said to her, 'The Holy Spirit will come upon you, and the
power of the Highest will overshadow you; therefore, also, that
Holy One who is to be born will be called the Son of God'"
(Luke 1:35).

Though Jesus was conceived of the Holy Spirit, He did not commence His public ministry of preaching, teaching, and working miracles until after He had been anointed with the Holy Spirit from on high. This took place when He was baptized in water by John the Baptist. "When He had been baptized, Jesus came up immediately from the water; and behold, the heavens were opened to Him, and He saw the Spirit of God descending like a dove and alighting upon Him" (Matt. 3:16). It is evident that He relied upon the Holy Spirit's anointing for power and for guidance in His ministry.

It is this understanding that prompts our concern and study about the importance of "the anointing" on a leader's life and ministry. Let's begin with Jesus as the Leader of leaders.

Read the following verses and note the way the Holy Spirit directed Jesus.

Luke 4:1, 2

Luke 4:14

Luke 4:16–21

 FAITH ALIVE

Jesus taught us to rely upon the Holy Spirit. With humility He said, "I can of Myself do nothing" (John 5:30). He set an example for those who lead when He expressed His need for the power of the Spirit to sustain Him. We, too, are to rely upon the Spirit's power and guidance so that we might accomplish the work He has for us.

What will happen in our ministries if we fail to rely upon the Holy Spirit's anointing?

The anointing of Jesus enabled Him to teach with authority (Matt. 7:29), to heal the centurion's servant (8:5–13), to cast out evil spirits (vv. 28–32), to perform miracles such as feeding the five thousand (14:15–21), to change water into wine (John 2:1–11), and to raise Lazarus from the dead (ch. 11). The wonderful works of Jesus are too numerous to mention. Yet in all of His ministry He acknowledged that He could do nothing apart from His Father. He clearly stated the purpose of the anointing that rested upon Him when He said:

> The Spirit of the Lord is upon Me, because He has anointed Me to preach the gospel to the poor; He has sent Me to heal the brokenhearted, to proclaim liberty to the captives and recovery of sight to the blind, to set at liberty those who are oppressed; to proclaim the acceptable year of the Lord (Luke 4:18, 19).

FULFILLMENT AND RESULTS OF THE PROMISED ANOINTING

Before Jesus ascended into heaven, He promised that He would pray to the Father to send the Helper (Holy Spirit) to His disciples, "And I will pray to the Father, and He will give you another Helper, that He may abide with you forever—the Spirit of truth, whom the world cannot receive, because it neither sees Him nor knows Him; but you know Him, for He dwells with you and will be in you" (John 14:16, 17).

His promise was fulfilled on the Day of Pentecost:

> When the Day of Pentecost had fully come, they [about 120 disciples] were all with one accord in one place. And suddenly there came a sound from heaven, as of a rushing mighty wind, and it filled the whole house where they were sitting. Then there appeared to them divided tongues, as of fire, and *one* sat upon each of them. And they were all filled with the Holy Spirit, and began to speak with other tongues, as the Spirit gave them utterance (Acts 2:1–4).

An outstanding trait that characterized the participants in the Pentecostal experience described in Acts 2:1–4 was boldness. Whereas the disciples had been fearful before, Peter, who had previously denied his Lord because of fear, now boldly preached the gospel of Christ (Acts 2:14–40), to the large crowd. What was the result?

WORD WEALTH

Boldness, *parrhesia* (par–rhay–*see*–ah), means outspokenness, unreserved utterance, freedom of speech, with frankness, candor, cheerful courage, and the opposite of cowardice, timidity or fear.[5]

FAITH ALIVE

Boldness in the faith characterizes those who are anointed by the Holy Spirit, "But you will receive power when the Holy Spirit has come upon you; and you shall be witnesses to Me in Jerusalem, and in all Judea and Samaria, and to the end of the earth" (Acts 1:8).

The Great Commission and the anointing go hand in hand. We all have a role to play in God's plan to reach the world with the gospel, but we are to go as anointed servants of God. Write in your responses to the following questions.

Do you feel adequate or inadequate to reach others for Christ? Describe your feelings.

On a scale of 1 to 10 (10 being the highest), how would you rate your reliance on the Holy Spirit? _____

Now put a check by the things most likely to keep you from relying upon the Holy Spirit:

__ Pride   __ My abilities

__ Self-confidence __ Other

__ Fear of failure __ Feeling that it all depends upon me

__ Doubt

What importance do you place upon waiting on the Lord in prayer so that you might be spiritually refreshed and anointed for ministry?

Describe ways in which you have experienced the power of God in your life to strengthen you for worship and ministry to Him.

The 120 believers who were tarrying in Jerusalem for the fulfillment of the Promise didn't know what to expect. But when the time was fully come, the Holy Spirit descended upon them and they were all filled with His presence and anointing.

As you discovered, there were several manifestations of the Holy Spirit on the Day of Pentecost, but there were two that stood out above the others. First, the 120 believers were enabled by the Spirit to speak with other tongues (Acts 2:4, 6–8).

   WORD WEALTH

Other tongues, *heterais glossais,* refers to spoken human languages, unknown to the speakers but known to the others (Acts 2:6).

A gift that developed later in the church is different kinds of tongues, *gene glosson* (I Cor. 12:10). It is the gift of speaking supernaturally in a language not known to the individual. When manifested in the public assembly, it is to be accompanied by the gift of interpretation of tongues (14:6–19).

The second outstanding manifestation on the Day of Pentecost was the anointed preaching of the gospel by Peter. As was previously mentioned, he who because of fear had denied his

Lord now preached in His name under the anointing of the Holy Spirit, with outstanding results. Yet the account of the outpouring on the Day of Pentecost does not cover the full scope of the Spirit's activity. The following references will give us a fuller understanding of how we may expect the Holy Spirit to work in the church today. Enter after each reference your findings about the Holy Spirit's workings.

John 14:26

John 16:7, 8

John 16:13

Acts 10:19, 20

Acts 13:2

Romans 8:14

1 Corinthians 12:7–11, 28

Galatians 5:22, 23

CONCLUSION

It seems appropriate to close this lesson by giving special consideration to anointed preaching and teaching. It merits special attention since the gifts of preaching and teaching incorporate in themselves many of the other gifts of the Spirit.

The gifts of the word of wisdom and the word of knowledge are often manifested in the exercise of anointed preaching and teaching. In an instant, the anointed preacher or teacher might find the gift of the discerning of spirits operating during a sermon or lesson, and this would enable him or her to address a critical need in the church body. Prophecy often accompanies the anointed preaching and teaching of the Word as well.

Ralph M. Riggs makes the following comment on preaching that is not anointed: "Preaching with wisdom of words, with enticing words of man's wisdom, or with excellency of speech which is purely natural, is as much an intrusion of the profane into the holy as an admission of a Canaanite into the house of the Lord of Hosts (see Zechariah 14:21)."[6] These comments could also apply to teaching.

The results of Peter's preaching to Cornelius's household has to be the dream of every anointed leader. Luke writes, "While Peter was still speaking these words, the Holy Spirit fell upon all those who heard the word. And those of the circumcision who believed were astonished, as many as came with Peter, because the gift of the Holy Spirit had been poured out on the Gentiles also" (Acts 10:44–46).

Anointed preaching and teaching bring results.

1. *Webster's Ninth New Collegiate Dictionary* (Springfield, MA, U.S.A.: Merriam-Webster Inc., Publishers, 1988).

2. *Spirit-Filled Life Bible* (Nashville, TN: Thomas Nelson Publishers, 1991), 1043, "Word Wealth: Isa. 61:1, anointed."

3. A. B. Simpson, *The Holy Spirit, Vol. 1, The Old Testament* (Harrisburg, PA: Christian Publications, Inc., no pub. date), 129–130.

4. *Spirit-Filled Life Bible*, 518–519, note on 1 Kin. 19:19.

5. Ibid., 1632, "Word Wealth: Acts 4:31, boldness."

6. Ralph M. Riggs, *The Spirit Himself* (Springfield, MO: The Gospel Publishing House, 1949), 178.

Lesson 9/Openness to Others

Have you ever had the humbling experience of taking the time to talk with someone, when you really didn't feel you had the time, and then hear that person say, "Oh, thank you for taking the time to talk with me! I feel as though a great load has been lifted. You have made my day!"? Humbling indeed. Your openness to someone in need cost you so little, but for that person, every minute you gave them was golden.

Being open and approachable to others is not the easiest of leadership traits to develop, for there is a tendency in all of us to want to protect ourselves—to be closed, defensive, and even judgmental.

To be open means to be vulnerable, having the ability to humbly share one's own struggles and victories and to be empathetic toward others. A leader who is open hides nothing and avoids being defensive. He or she is accessible, available, and transparent.

Pride and exclusivity are traits opposite to openness. They prevent leaders from developing nurturing relationships with those they lead and often form leaders who work at projecting power by whatever means they might, even through intimidation.

Some leadership models used in the corporate world make it next to impossible for leaders to function with openness. Such models distance the leaders from those being led. Developing personal relationships under such models is difficult.

Trained lay leadership can help to provide a more approachable and accessible extension of pastoral care under the corporate model. But when the skills of trained lay leadership are inadequate to deal with the more complex spiritual issues, then there must be made available to the congregation trained pastoral staff to minister to those areas.

There is probably no perfect leadership model available to the church today. But those who aspire to be Christlike in their leadership should strive to be open, approachable people.

OPENNESS MODELED IN CHRIST

The Gospels are full of accounts that reveal the openness and approachableness of Christ. People with insurmountable problems and physical needs followed Him wherever He went. He took the time to listen to their needs and respond to them compassionately. So secure was He in His own personal identity and mission that He could make Himself available to the people. Instead of distancing Himself, He invited them to come to Him with all their problems. He said, "Come to Me, all you who labor and are heavy laden, and I will give you rest" (Matt. 11:28).

The following Bible passages provide insights into the openness of Jesus. After reading the passages, record in the respective columns the setting and the manner in which Jesus responded to the need and how that response revealed His openness to the people.

	Setting	Manner of Jesus' Response	How Jesus' Openness Was Revealed
Matt. 15:32–39			
Matt. 20:29–34			
Mark 7:24–30			
Mark 10:9, 13–16			
Luke 19:1–9			
John 4:3–30, 39–41			

FAITH ALIVE

The following will help you learn to apply in your ministry some lessons from the above examples of Jesus' accessibility to the people.

Feeding the Four Thousand:
Prior to the miracle of the feeding of the four thousand, how much time had Jesus spent with the multitude and how must He have felt physically after that length of time?

What did the disciples learn about leadership as a result of their participation in this miracle?

How can you apply the lessons they learned to your own ministry?

Two Blind Men:
What can you learn from the persistence of the two blind men?

As a leader, have you ever become impatient with someone who was persistent in his or her desire to receive ministry when the circumstances at the moment did not lend to giving this person the attention he or she felt was needed?

What does Jesus' response to the blind men teach us?

Syro-Phoenician Woman:
What do we learn in this story about being responsive to people whose needs are so desperate that they seem to violate the rules of protocol to get help?

Do you desire to be the kind of person that someone who is in critical need would feel free to call for help, even at what seems to be the most inopportune time? If so, note any ways you may need to change so that you might become more approachable.

Jesus Blessing the Children:
Why do you suppose the disciples wanted to keep the little children away from Jesus?

What does this tell you about their understanding of a leader's accessibility at that point in their discipleship training?

In what ways do you think spiritual leaders should demonstrate their love and concerns for children today?

Jesus Visiting Zacchaeus's House:
What lesson can be learned from Jesus taking the initiative to invite Himself to Zacchaeus's house?

How would you handle the criticism Jesus received for going to his home?

What about the time element involved in Jesus' visit, and what message about ministry does this communicate to us?

The Woman of Samaria:
In what ways was this an unusual encounter?

What is Jesus teaching us about our accessibility to people who are considered outcasts in society?

OPENNESS MODELED IN PAUL

Ordinarily the apostle Paul did not boast about his apostolic gifts or the successes of his ministry. Nor did he boast of the incredible sufferings he endured in his service to Christ. No other apostle was more gifted than Paul, nor did any of them suffer to the extent that he did. But when writing his second letter to the Corinthians, he found it necessary to become "boastful" to the point of appearing foolish in doing so. In this epistle, Paul revealed details about the sufferings he endured as an apostle. He also reminded the Corinthians of his sacrificial ministry to them. All of this personal revelation was necessary so that the Christians at Corinth might compare his calling and experiences with those who claimed to be apostles but who, in fact, were not.

To discover the degree of vulnerability demonstrated by Paul to the church at Corinth, read 2 Corinthians 11 and 12, and then from the following divisions within those chapters (listed in the left column), record the struggles of this great leader in the right column.

2 Corinthians	Paul's Vulnerability	His Struggles
11:1–4		
11:5–15		
11:16–21		
11:22–33		

2 Corinthians	Paul's Vulnerability	His Struggles
12:1–6		
12:7–10		
12:11–13		
12:14–21		

OPENNESS TO WISE COUNSEL

Solomon saw the value of wise counsel when he wrote, "Without counsel, plans go awry, but in the multitude of counselors they are established" (Prov. 15:22).

One of the causes for failure in leadership is the unwillingness to be open to wise counsel. Costly mistakes can be avoided when one will seek the advice of experienced, successful leaders.

Openness to wise counsel will lead to accountability. Persons in places of leadership must be accountable to others. Pastors are accountable to church boards, their congregations, and ecclesiastical overseers. They do not operate independently. Those in places of spiritual leadership should learn to be team players as well as leaders. Regularly scheduled meetings, retreats, and training sessions provide opportunities for members of the leadership team to receive wise counsel and to be accountable to one another.

MOSES RECEIVES COUNSEL

An example of a great spiritual leader who is open to wise counsel is found in Exodus 18. Read the entire chapter and then answer the following questions.

How would you describe the relationship between Moses and his father-in-law, Jethro?

What were the qualities Jethro possessed that would give him the right to offer counsel to Moses?

What is the value of open-minded dialogue in counsel?

Describe Moses' response to wise counsel, how he personally benefited by it, and how the people benefited.

What negative results might have happened had not Moses been open to receive his father-in-law's wise counsel?

 FAITH ALIVE

To help you apply the truths of "openness" to your ministry, respond to the following items:

Rate your first reaction to wise counsel.

__ Defensive   __ Threatened   __ Open

If you are defensive or feel threatened, twhy do you feel like this?

OPENNESS ENCOURAGES ECUMENISM

The body of Christ encompasses many denominations and independent groups. There are also many different liturgical expressions of worship and service in the various church fellowships. But the true church is one body, and Christ cannot be divided. He prayed that we all may be one (John 17:21). It is a powerful testimony to the world when believers from the various Christian traditions come together in unity. It is especially desirable that Christian leaders be open to the spirit of unity and true ecumenism.

WORD WEALTH

Ecumenical, *oikoumenikos,* means 1) worldwide or general in extent, influence, or application; 2a.) of, relating to, or representing the whole of a body of churches; b.) promoting or tending toward worldwide Christian unity or cooperation.

"Ecumenism" speaks of ecumenical principles and practices especially as shown among religious groups (as Christian denominations).[1]

Paul demonstrated an ecumenical spirit when he wrote, "For I long to see you, that I may impart to you some spiritual gift so that you may be established—that is, that I might be encouraged together with you by the *mutual faith both of you and me*" (Rom. 1:11, 12; emphasis added).

Mutuality of the faith is to be honored in the Christian community at large. No one segment of the church of Jesus Christ has exclusive rights or claim to the faith. Faith in the person and work of Jesus Christ is the cement that holds true believers of all traditions together in Christian fellowship.

Read John 17:20–26, and record your thoughts about true ecumenism.

In this prayer to the Father, Jesus prayed for the unity of believers in all succeeding generations. What evidence do you see in the world today that His prayer is being answered?

Of what value is open-mindedness in spiritual leaders for achieving such ecumenism?

Is ecumenism achievable in this life, or are we "rushing heaven?"

   FAITH ALIVE

Review here what you have learned from studying the scriptures pertaining to ecumenism.

List areas in your life where you need to apply the truths or principles learned.

What do you feel to be the basic or fundamental confession of faith that serves to bind all true believers together?

How far should one go with open-mindedness when it comes to joining in fellowship with those of other traditions whose worship and service to Christ differ in practice than one's own?

Of what importance is it that the nonChrisian world see a truly ecumenical spirit among true believers? In you?

OPENNESS AND EVANGELISM

After His resurrection Jesus Christ commissioned His followers to go into all the world and make disciples of all nations (Matt. 28:18–20). Luke adds these words, spoken by Jesus just before His ascension, "But you shall receive power when the Holy Spirit has come upon you; and you shall be witnesses to Me in Jerusalem, and in all Judea, and Samaria, and to the end of the earth" (Acts 1:8). They were to start at Jerusalem, and then in ever-widening circles they were to increase the scope of their witness until the entire world had been evangelized.

Yet there were certain obstacles in disciples' minds that had to be dealt with, obstacles that would hinder them from fulfilling the Great Commission. Perhaps the greatest of these was the hatred that existed between the Jews and the Gentiles. How could these newly commissioned Jewish evangelists possibly take the gospel to a people for whom they had no respect and whose cultural practices were contrary to their Jewish traditions? Peter is an example of how this is possible.

Peter Breaks through Cultural Barriers

Read Leviticus 11:4–7, 13–19, 29–30. These verses speak of the animals and birds which the Jews were to exclude from their diet. They were considered to be ritually unclean and not to be eaten.

Read also Acts 10:9–16, 34. Note that Peter was commanded to rise, kill, and eat of the ritually unclean animals shown to him in the vision. This vision was repeated three times, but he refused to do so because he had never eaten anything unclean. To have killed and eaten anything unclean would have been a violation of his Jewish tradition.

Yet notice particularly verse 15, "A voice spoke to him again the second time, 'What God has cleansed you must not call common.'" This vision was intended to show Peter that God is no respecter of persons. Verse 34 makes it clear, "Then Peter opened his mouth and said: 'In truth I perceive that God shows no partiality.'"

Review Acts 10, and answer from the passage the following questions, keeping in mind that the emphasis in this section is on openness and evangelism.

What sort of man was Cornelius?

How do you suppose Cornelius came to know God in such a personal way?

Cornelius was a Gentile soldier in the occupying Roman army. What might we find surprising about his open relationship with the Jews?

Why do you suppose Peter was shown the vision three times?

What feelings might Peter have experienced when Cornelius's messengers presented themselves at his gate?

Describe what Peter and Cornelius each must have felt as they finally stood face-to-face.

What evidence do we have that Peter's heart was truly opened to Cornelius and the other Gentiles gathered at Cornelius's house?

What extraordinary event happened as Peter preached the gospel to the Gentiles gathered at Cornelius's house, and what was the response of the Jews who had come with Peter when they witnessed this event?

 FAITH ALIVE

List the cultural barriers that exist in the area where you live and how these barriers hinder evangelism in your community.

What cultural barriers are you struggling to break through? Make this a matter of prayer, asking God to help you to be open and accepting of all people so that you might be a channel He can use to reach people of other cultures with the gospel.

SUMMARY

In this lesson we have seen openness to others as it was modeled in the lives and ministries of Jesus and the apostles Peter and Paul. We have also seen the value of being open to wise counsel. And we learned that if unity among believers is to become a reality, then there must be openness to those of the Christian faith who may not be of our own denomination or tradition. This openness to others is also essential to the ministry of evangelism.

Openness to others is the key to unity in the body of Christ and to world evangelism. Let God use this key in your life to effect change in your world!

1. *Webster's Ninth New Collegiate Dictionary* (Springfield, MA: U.S.A.: Merriam-Webster Inc., Publishers, 1988).

Lesson 10/Dependence on God

The teacher of a Sunday school class of junior boys was concerned that each of his students come to know Christ as Savior. In spite of the lesson preparations he would make during the week and the fun activities he provided for them, their interest in spiritual things seemed to lag. He tried everything. It was not until he resorted to a time of fasting and prayer, praying earnestly for each of them by name, that a change came. The interest of the boys picked up, and there were fewer distractions in the class. Then, over a period of a few weeks, the teacher saw the rewards of his dependence upon God as each of his students accepted Christ as Savior.

Spiritual leaders today are faced with a variety of challenges. Some of those challenges are extraordinary in nature and require special grace and blessing from God if they are to be met successfully. Those who engage in fasting and prayer give evidence of dependence upon God and may be assured that what they need will be supplied.

Those who exercise these disciplines show their dependence upon God for direction in their personal lives and in their ministries.

JESUS OUR EXAMPLE IN PRAYER

Our great example, Jesus the Son of God, was preeminently a man of prayer. He prayed often. He prayed early in the morning, and there is at least one recorded occasion when He prayed all night. He prayed when His life was in danger. He prayed before making important decisions, such as deciding who His twelve apostles would be. And Jesus taught His disciples to pray. Since then, all of God's greatest men and women have been people of prayer.

Mark records one of Jesus' morning prayers, "Now in the morning, having risen a long time before daylight, He went out and departed to a solitary place; and there He prayed" (Mark 1:35). After that time of prayer Jesus commenced an extended ministry in Galilee. Mark tells us, "He was preaching in their synagogues throughout all Galilee, and casting out demons" (v. 39). It is apparent that Jesus depended upon the Father to give Him strength and direction for His ministry through prayer.

 FAITH ALIVE

Read Mark 1:32–34. What do these verses tell us about the intensity of Jesus' ministry the night before His early morning time of prayer?

What principle do you see at work in the life of Jesus at this point that spiritual leaders should apply in their lives today?

Luke's Gospel tells us about Jesus spending all night in prayer, "And it came to pass in those days that He went out to the mountain to pray, and continued all night in prayer to God" (6:12). This means He probably went all night without sleep. That is serious praying! But for Jesus, the decisions He had to make warranted serious praying; He was about to choose His twelve disciples.

On the night of His betrayal in the garden of Gethsemane, Jesus spent time in agonizing prayer, "And being in agony, He prayed more earnestly" (Luke 22:44).

In that time of prayer, He yielded Himself to the Father, saying, "Nevertheless not My will, but Yours, be done" (v. 42). It was in prayer that He found the grace and strength to make the ultimate sacrifice, the giving of His life so that others might have eternal life.

FAITH ALIVE

We all experience "Gethsemanes." When have you faced a crisis that brought you to a place of agonizing prayer? What was the nature of the crisis?

What were your feelings as you came face-to-face with the crisis? Feelings of inadequacy? Anger? Fear?

Did you wrestle with the issue of your will or God's will being done? Did you receive grace from God that enabled you to say, "Not my will but Yours be done"?

What has been God's direction in your life since?

Prayer did not cease in the life of our Lord after His agony in Gethsemane. Later He prayed for those who nailed Him to the cross saying, "Father, forgive them, for they do not know what they do" (Luke 23:34). Crucifixion was an extremely painful way to be put to death. Yet, in His infinite love, Jesus prayed for forgiveness for those who put Him on the Cross.

FAITH ALIVE

Those who lead in the church must prayerfully forgive those who offend them. Offenses come to leaders; they are inescapable. Some offenses hurt a lot. But leaders must pray with forgiveness from the heart for those who spitefully use them and say all manner of evil against them. God will hear and answer that prayer.

Write a prayer to Jesus expressing your gratitude to Him for dying on the Cross for you and for forgiving your sins.

Write a second prayer in which you express your forgiveness of those who have hurt you. Thank Him for setting the example of forgiveness in prayer.

While suspended on the Cross, Jesus prayed other prayers. One was of inquiry, "Eli, Eli, lama sabachthani?" that is, "My God, My God, why have You forsaken me?" (Matt. 27:46). Another was one of commitment, "Father, into Your hands I commit My spirit" (Luke 23:46).

Jesus' prayers from the Cross were not to be the last He would pray. We are told in Scripture that Jesus is now in the presence of the Father praying for us, "Therefore He is also able to save to the uttermost those who come to God through Him, since He always lives to make intercession for them" (Heb. 7:25).

 WORD WEALTH

Make intercession, *entunchano* (en–toong–*khan*–oh), means to fall in with, meet in order to converse. From this description of a casual encounter, the word progresses to the idea of pleading with a person on behalf of another, although at times the petition may be against another (Acts 25:24; Rom. 11:2).[1]

PRAYER IN A LEADER'S LIFE

It is blessed to know that Jesus is in heaven praying for us. It means that He is alive and sensitive to our needs. He was tested and tempted just as we are, so He can be touched with our weaknesses (Heb. 4:15).

But Jesus has given us the responsibility and privilege of prayer too. One day Jesus' disciples asked Him to teach them to pray (Luke 11:1). In response to their request, Jesus gave them a prayer that has come to be known as "The Lord's Prayer" or the "Our Father" prayer (Matt. 6:9–13). This prayer can be prayed not only from memory in private or public situations, but it also furnishes a model or pattern for prayer. The ingredients for good praying are to be found in it, and from it other prayers can be developed.

Consider the following five ways leaders can grow in prayer.

1. *By praying.* Just as practice brings improvement in music or sports, just so practice brings improvement in praying.

2. *By meditating on Scripture.* Someone has said, "Meditation is the missing link between Bible intake and prayer." Meditating on the Scriptures builds our faith so that we are able to believe God when we pray. The humanly impossible becomes possible through faith in God and prayer.

3. *By praying with other people* who can model true prayer for them.

4. *By reading about those who excelled in their prayer lives* and as a result were able to see God do extraordinary things.

5. *As they see their prayers answered.* God does not tell us to pray in a wishful manner. When He tells us to ask, seek, and knock, Jesus means to answer us.

Reflect on each of these ways to grow in prayer, and write specific ways you can imagine applying each in your life.

BASIC ELEMENTS OF PRAYER

There are certain basic elements of prayer that are revealed in the following Bible verses. Read the verses and identify in center column the type of prayer being used, such as: Confession, gratitude, petition or supplication, intercession, and worship or adoration. Then circle in the right column how frequently you use that particular kind of prayer in your own prayer life.

Reference	Type	My Frequency of Use		
		Often	Sometimes	Rarely
Ps. 100:4, 5		O	S	R
Luke 1:46, 47		O	S	R
Phil. 4:6		O	S	R
1 Tim. 2:1–4		O	S	R
1 John 1:8, 9		O	S	R

DEVELOPING AN EFFECTIVE PRAYER LIFE

Listed below are some helps toward developing an effective prayer life.

• *Maintain a right relationship with God*
A right relationship with God has been made possible through Christ's work of redemption for us. Paul writes, "Therefore being justified by faith, we have peace with God through our Lord Jesus Christ" (Rom. 5:1). If we seem to be failing in our prayer lives, perhaps there are things that are blocking the answers from coming through.

Read the following passages of Scripture listed below and list possible causes of ineffective prayer.

Causes of Ineffective Prayer

Deuteronomy 1:34–45

Psalm 66:18

Proverbs 1:28, 29   **Causes of Ineffective Prayer**

Isaiah 59:2

James 1:6, 7

James 4:3

• *Maintain right relationships with others*
  Read Matthew 5:23, 24, and note how these verses instruct
us with regard to maintaining right relationships with others.

• *Repentance from sin*
  Read Psalm 66:18, and note how sin in the heart affects
our prayers.

• *Exercise faith in prayer*
  Read Matthew 7:8, and describe what wonderful promises
this verse provides for those who pray.

     Charles Haddon Spurgeon said, "I cannot imagine any one
of you tantalizing your child by exciting in him a desire that you
did not intend to gratify. It were a very ungenerous thing to
offer alms to the poor, and then when they hold out their hand

for it to mock their poverty with a denial. It were a cruel addition to the miseries of the sick if they were taken to the hospital and there left to die untended and uncared for. Where God leads you to pray, He means you to receive."[2]

- *Seek God's will when you pray*
Read Luke 22:42, and describe what this verse teaches about submission to God in prayer.

SPIRITUAL WARFARE

Frequent mention is made of Satan, powers, and principalities in the Pauline epistles. It is clear from Paul's writings that Satan and his evil host are in open rebellion against God and seek to attack and defeat God's people. Spiritual leaders are to be knowledgeable of the ways in which these adversaries of God work and how to engage in warfare against them.

These powers penetrate all cultures and social structures, seeking to enslave people in legalism, mysticism, and superstition. They blind people from the truth. They are the rulers of this present darkness (Eph. 6:12). They crucified the Lord of glory (1 Cor. 2:8). They keep people from the love of God. Spiritual leaders must contend with them.

Cosmic war rages between God and Satan and it is impossible for mankind to escape it. However, we can choose which side we want to be on, God's or Satan's. Choosing Christ as Savior and Lord puts us on God's side, the winning side. Jesus' purpose for coming into the world was to destroy the works of the devil (1 John 3:8). And He accomplished what He came to do!

In the following scriptures you will discover what Christ accomplished in His death. Enter the accomplishment after each reference.

1 Corinthians 15:27, 28

Colossians 2:15

1 John 3:8

1 John 2:2

THE ARMOR OF GOD

Though the conflict continues, we have the armor of God with which to do battle against the enemy (Eph. 6:10–17). We are instructed to put the armor on so that we may be able to stand against the wiles of the devil and to withstand the evil day (vv. 11, 13). The armor is totally adequate, but for it to be effective we must put it on.

What do you understand Paul to mean by each of the six pieces of armor he lists in Ephesians 6:14–17?

How are we to put the armor on?

THE PLACE OF PRAYER IN SPIRITUAL WARFARE

After describing the armor of God, Paul speaks of prayer, "Praying always with all prayer and supplication in the Spirit, being watchful to this end with all perseverance and supplication for all the saints" (Eph. 6:18).

"Thus, prayer is not so much a weapon, or even a part of the armor, as it is the means by which we engage in the battle itself and the purpose for which we are armed. To put on the armor of God is to prepare for battle. Prayer is the battle itself, with God's Word being our chief weapon employed against Satan during our struggle."[3]

Paul, great spiritual leader that he was, did not hesitate to request prayer of the Christians at Ephesus, "and [pray] for me, that utterance may be given to me, that I may open my mouth boldly to make known the mystery of the gospel" (Eph. 6:19). If the apostle Paul needed prayer for the ministry, then surely all who are in places of leadership today need prayer no less than he. Spiritual leaders, because of their position on the front lines of battle, need the support of men and women who know how to pray.

Read Ephesians 1:19–21.

Where do these verses tell us Christ is now?

What do they say of His exaltation?

Of what significance is His exaltation to us who are in spiritual conflict here on earth?

FASTING

To fast is to abstain from food. Fasting has, in all ages and among all nations, been much in use in times of mourning, sorrow, and affliction. There are no examples of fasting to be seen before Moses. Leviticus 23:27 tells us of fasting that was observed on the Day of Atonement. Joshua 7:6 tells us of Joshua and the elders laying prostrate before the Lord from morning to evening without taking food, after Israel had been defeated in their attempt to take the city of Ai. David fasted while the first child he had by Bathsheba was sick (2 Sam. 12:16).

Moses fasted forty days on Mount Horeb (Ex. 34:28). First Kings 19:8 tells us Elijah went forty days without eating. Jesus fasted in the wilderness for forty days and forty nights (Matt. 4:2). All of these fasts were extraordinary. Such extended fasts are not recorded elsewhere in Scripture.

Jesus did not institute any particular fasts. But the inference of such scriptures as Luke 5:33–35 is that His disciples would fast. The one condition that He made was that they be sincere (Matt. 6:17, 18).

Jesus' instruction to His disciples that they be sincere and private in their times of fasting was to set them apart from the hypocritical pretenders, who paraded their fastings with sad, austere faces to be seen of men. By contrast, the disciples were not to advertise their piety. All forms of self-denial were to be secret and without show.

Read the following Bible verses and fill in each column with the appropriate response.

	Occasion for Fast	Participants	Divine Promise
Joel 1:13–20			
Joel 2:12–14			
Matt. 6:17, 18			
Matt. 17:21			

The following Bible verses provide further examples of fasting. After reading the verses in their context, enter as in the previous exercise the occasion for the fast and those who were involved.

	Occasion for Fast	Participants
Exodus 34:28		
1 Samuel 7:6		
1 Kings 19:8		

	Occasion for Fast	Participants
Ezra 10:6		
Daniel 10:3		
Luke 4:1, 2		
Acts 9:1–9		
Acts 13:2, 3		
Acts 14:23		

CONCLUSION

"Leaders of the early church arrived at decisions only after fasting and prayer. In Antioch the prophets and teachers fasted and prayed, seeking God's direction for the church. While they waited on God, the Holy Spirit gave direction (v. 2), thus beginning the missionary ministry, which eventually took the gospel to the whole world. Godly leaders rely on God for the direction and the empowering of their lives and ministry. Disciplined fasting and constant prayer are proven means for this, and as such, are mandatory in the lives of leaders (Matt. 9:15)."[4]

---

1. *Spirit-Filled Life Bible* (Nashville, TN: Thomas Nelson Publishers, 1991), 1880, "Word Wealth: Heb. 7:25, make intercession."

2. C.H. Spurgeon, "Thought-Reading Extraordinary," *Metropolitan Tabernacle Pulpit, Vol. 30* (London: Passmore and Alabaster, 1885; reprint, Pasadena, TX: Pilgrim Publications, 1973), 539–540.

3. *Spirit-Filled Life Bible*, 1797, "Kingdom Dynamics: Eph. 6:10, Spiritual Warfare."

4. Ibid., 1650, "Kingdom Dynamics: Acts 13:1–3, Fasting and Prayer."

Lesson 11/Belief in Miracles, Signs, and Wonders

This lesson assumes that spiritual leaders believe in miracles, signs, and wonders. From the opening verses of Genesis, which deal with Creation, to the closing verses of the book of Revelation, which deal with the coming of the Lord and the new Creation, there is evidence of the miraculous. The Old Testament records miracles that took place under the leadership of Moses and Aaron (Ex. 4:3, 9, 30; 7:10, 20); Joshua (Josh. 3:6; 10:12); Samson (Judg. 14:6, 19; 16:3); Samuel (1 Sam. 12:18); Elijah (1 Kin. 17:1, 14, 22); Elisha (2 Kin. 2:14, 21, 24; 3:16); and Isaiah (2 Kin. 20:7, 11).

In the New Testament, all four Gospel writers speak of at least thirty-seven miracles Jesus performed, e.g., healings (Matt. 8:14; Mark 1:31), raising the dead (Luke 7:11; John 11), feeding five thousand people with a few loaves and fishes (John 6:5), walking on the water (Matt. 14:26, 27), casting out devils (12:22), calming storms with a spoken word (8:26), cleansing lepers (v. 3), and opening blind eyes and deaf ears (Matt. 9:27; Mark 7:37).

The apostle Peter performed miracles, as recorded in Acts 3:7; 5:5, 10, 15; 9:34. The miracles of Paul are recorded in Acts 13:11; 14:3, 10; 16:18; 19:11; 20:10; 28:5. Miracles were also performed by the seventy (Luke 10:17), by Stephen (Acts 6:8), and by Philip (8:6–13).

In this lesson, we will consider: 1) miracles, signs, and wonders in the Old and New Testaments; 2) the purpose for miracles, signs, and wonders; 3) the truth that they are for today; and 4) the need to discern the source of miracles.

MIRACLES, SIGNS, AND WONDERS IN THE OLD TESTAMENT

WORD WEALTH

Miracles. A number of Hebrew, Aramaic, and Greek words are used in the Bible to refer to God's activity in nature and history. They are variously translated in English as "miracles," "wonders," "signs," "mighty acts," "powers." Thus, for example, the Hebrew word *mopet,* which is of uncertain etymology, is translated in AV [*Authorized Version*] by "miracle" (Ex. 7:9; Deut. 24:3), "wonder" (e.g., Ex. 7:3; Deut. 4:34; Ps. 78:43), and "sign" (e.g., 1 Ki. 13:3, 5).[1]

Works of God. When the word "sign" is used in the plural together with "wonders" (*mopet*), the events are understood to be the works of God, or attestation of His active presence among His people. This is seen in Exodus, where the plagues are described as signs (Ex. 4:28; 7:3; 8:23); the Exodus itself with the deaths of the Egyptian first-born, the crossing of the Red Sea, and the destruction of the Egyptian army, provides the supreme example of such signs and wonders (Deut. 4:34, 6:22, 7:19). This conviction is found throughout the Old Testament (e.g., Josh. 24:17; Ps.78:43; Jer. 32:21; Neh. 9:10), and Israel was assured that when God revealed Himself again it would be with "signs and wonders" to herald His coming (Joel 2:30)."[2]

THE PURPOSE OF MIRACLES, SIGNS, AND WONDERS

The purpose of miracles, signs, and wonders is that men might know the power of God. In all the following settings, God performed mighty works so that all men might know His power.

MOSES

God gave Moses many miraculous signs in preparation to lead Israel out of Egyptian slavery. To discover the nature of these miracles, read the verses in the left column. Then describe in the other three columns the nature of each miracle, the purpose of the miracle, and the sense in which each miracle had relevance to God's call upon Moses' life.

Signs and Miracles
In Preparation for Moses' Assignment

Exodus	Nature of Miracle	Purpose	How Relevant to Call of Moses
4:1–5			
4:6–8			
4:9			

 FAITH ALIVE

God works in a variety of ways in the lives of those whom He calls to leadership. Everyone has a personal testimony of how God initiated that call, and how He has worked since. In some instances God works miraculously or through signs and wonders to effect the call.

In the space provided write down: 1) how God called you into His service; 2) His dealings with you now in your place of ministry; and 3) any miracle, sign, or wonder that God might have used to effect His call in your life.

God's Call to His Service

God at Work in My Ministry Today

Extraordinary Event that Effected My Call

MOSES AND AARON

God not only proved Himself to Moses. He continued to perform signs and wonders through Moses and his spokesman and brother, Aaron (4:10–17). God worked great signs and wonders in the land of Egypt so that the Egyptians might know that He was Lord. To discover how God worked miracles through these brothers, read the following scriptures listed in the left column which deal with the ten plagues God brought on the Egyptians. Enter in the other columns the nature of each miracle and its effect upon the Egyptians.

Exodus	Nature of Miracle	Effect upon the Egyptians
7:20		
8:6, 13		
8:17		
8:21, 31		
9:3		
9:10		
9:23		

Exodus	Nature of Miracle	Effect upon the Egyptians
10:13, 19		
10:22		
12:29		

PASSOVER

This important event in Israel's history represents deliverance and new beginnings: deliverance from Egyptian slavery and new beginnings as a nation. Read the passage (Exod. 12:1–13), which records this dramatic event.

For Israel, the blood of a slain lamb applied to the doorposts and the lintels of their homes would be a sign to the death angel to pass over and not slay their firstborn. It was the blood that protected them.

The Passover is a symbol of Christ our Redeemer, the Lamb of God who shed His blood for the sins of the world. Those who trust in Him as Savior are delivered from the bondage of sin and are given a new beginning, a new life in Him.

"Therefore purge out the old leaven, that you may be a new lump, since you truly are unleavened. For indeed Christ, our Passover, was sacrificed for us" (1 Cor. 5:7).

 FAITH ALIVE

All believers will agree that the greatest miracle in one's life is the miracle of the rebirth—that experience when God, seeing the blood of His Son applied to a sinner's heart, passes over our sin and grants cleansing and eternal life instead of judgment.

Write about your "Passover" experience, when Christ came into your heart, granting you new life instead of judgment.

Express in writing your appreciation for Christ's blood.

RED SEA CROSSING

The first real test of Israel's faith takes place during their escape from Egypt. The Israelites panicked upon finding themselves with their backs to Pharaoh's army and an uncrossable body of water before them.

Read Exodus 14:1—15:1 to discover how God proved to Israel that all they needed to do was stand still and see His salvation.

 ### FAITH ALIVE

We seem to need miracles almost every day of our lives. Do you feel that you are "between the devil and the deep blue sea?" Is there a pursuing enemy after you?

What battle do you need God to fight for you in the days ahead?

Have you ever faced a crisis when God told you to stand still and see His salvation, but like the Israelites you wanted to turn back? Put a check by any of the following conditions that may have contributed to your fears and failure to trust God.

__ Was a new believer

__ Lack of knowledge of God's Word

__ Knew God's promises but chose not to believe them

__ Did not believe God would come through

__ Trusted in own abilities and wisdom

__ Out of fellowship with God and His people

Many people today are facing "Red Sea crossings"—real tests and crises in their lives. Read Genesis 18:14; Jeremiah 32:17, 27; Matthew 19:26; and Hebrews 13:8. Do you believe that God can deliver today as He did in Bible times?

If there are some doubts in your mind, list the steps you must take to reach a place of total trust in God for times of crises.

How can a leader be a help to those he or she is leading who are facing a crisis?

THE WILDERNESS

Throughout Israel's wilderness wanderings, God continued to manifest His power to His people through miracles. As you read the following Scripture, briefly note the mood of the people, nature of each miracle, and what effect the miracle had on the people involved.

The Water Sweetened
Exodus 15:22–25

Mood of the People   **Nature of Miracle**   **Effect upon People**

 FAITH ALIVE

Just three days into their journey from Egypt, Israel found no fresh water to drink. It was their first major test after crossing the Red Sea. They grumbled against Moses and said, "What shall we drink?" (Ex. 15:24).

To whom were the people looking for provision—to God or to their leader, Moses?

Had you been the leader of these people, what would you have done had they come to you with their complaint?

What did Moses do in response to the complaint of the people, which proved his dependence upon God and his ability to lead?

What "bittersweet" experience have you had recently? How did God sweeten the water for you?

MIRACLES, SIGNS, AND WONDERS IN THE NEW TESTAMENT

The pages of the New Testament are filled with miracles, signs, and wonders. In the opening chapter of Matthew, the first miracle recorded is that of the conception of Jesus by the Holy Spirit in the womb of a virgin named Mary (Matt. 1:18). Followed by the birth of Christ and the miracles, signs, and wonders that accompanied His birth, the four Gospels continue to record the many miracles performed by Christ. When the church was birthed in the book of Acts, miracles, signs, and wonders continued to take place. And Revelation, the final book of the Bible, speaks of miracles, signs, and wonders that are yet to take place but will someday happen.

 WORD WEALTH

Miracle, *dunamis* (*doo*-nam-is), means: force (literal or figurative); special miraculous power (usually by implication a miracle itself): ability, abundance, meaning, might (-ily, -y, -y deed), (worker of) miracle(s), power, strength, violence, mighty (wonderful) work.[3]

Sign, *semeion* (say-*mi*-on), means: an indication or supernatural: miracle, sign, token, wonder.[4]

Wonder, *teras* (*teh*-ras), means: a prodigy or omen: wonder.[5]

MIRACLES OF CHRIST

It is clear from the Gospel of John that Jesus did many more things than are recorded in the Bible. In the last verse of his Gospel, John wrote, "And there are also many other things that Jesus did, which if they were written one by one, I suppose that even the world itself could not contain the books that would be written" (21:25). But in His wisdom the Holy Spirit included those miracles in the Gospels that would best serve His church in preparation for ministry and building up the faith.

Each of the following passages tell of a miracle of Christ. Read each one, then note the nature of the miracle, the people who especially benefited by the miracle, and how Jesus was perceived by the people after He had worked the miracle.

Water Turned to Wine
John 2:1–11

Nature of Miracle	Those Benefited by Miracle	People's Perception of Jesus

Jesus, who worked this miracle in Cana, continues His miracle ministry in the world today. All whom He touches by His Spirit are transformed. He transforms sinners into saints, darkness into light, despair into hope, sadness into joy. He will finally transform old heavens and earth into new heavens and a new earth (2 Pet. 3:7, 10).

Miraculous Drought of Fishes
Luke 5:1–11

Nature of Miracle	Those Benefited by Miracle	People's Perception of Jesus

FAITH ALIVE

When the fishermen saw the miraculous catch of fish and then heard the call of Jesus to follow Him, what do you suppose went through their minds?

In your call to serve Jesus, did it take an extraordinary event or the witnessing of a miracle to cause you to leave all and follow Him? If so, write about the experience.

Calming the Storm
Matthew 8:23–27; Mark 4:35–41; Luke 8:22–25

Nature of Miracle	Those Benefited by Miracle	People's Perception of Jesus

 FAITH ALIVE

How do you react when you are experiencing a circumstantial storm?

What part does prayer play when you are in the storm?

Does it sometimes seem to you that the Lord is asleep? If so, why does it seem that way?

What does this incident tell us about a miracle-working God?

The Demon–possessed Delivered
Matthew 8:28–34; Mark 5:1–20

Nature of Miracle	Those Benefited by Miracle	People's Perception of Jesus

WORD WEALTH

Demon, *daimonion* (die-*mon*-ion), means a demon, evil spirit; or by extension, a deity: devil, god.

Demon possession, *daimonidzomai* (die-mon-*idz*-omai), means: to be possessed, vexed, or afflicted by a demon; to be exercised by a demon.[6]

This miracle of Christ displayed His power over not just one demon but a legion of demons. At full strength a Roman legion was 6,000 in number. The name signified a well-organized military group having great power. Jesus confronted the legion of demons with a command that they come out of the man, and they immediately obeyed. They went into a herd of about 2,000 swine that was nearby. The swine ran down a steep place and into the sea where they were all drowned.

 FAITH ALIVE

What do we learn about Jesus in this miracle?

What do we learn about demons?

Why should people in places of spiritual leadership avail themselves of information regarding demons, demon possession, demon influence, and exorcism?

Of what importance is the name of Jesus in dealing with the enemy? (Mark 16:17)

SIGNS AND WONDERS OF THE APOSTLES

Jesus promised His disciples that signs would follow those who believe, "And these signs will follow those who believe: In My name they will cast out demons; they will speak with new tongues; they will take up serpents; and if they drink anything deadly, it will by no means hurt them; they will lay hands on the sick, and they will recover" (Mark 16:17, 18). We see this promise fulfilled particularly in the ministries of Peter and Paul.

Miracles of Peter

Acts	Nature of Miracle	Effect upon People
3:7		
5:5, 10		
5:15		

Miracles of Paul

Acts	Nature of Miracle	Effect upon People
13:11		
14:10		
16:18		

MIRACLES, SIGNS, AND WONDERS TODAY

Though there are arguments that miracles, signs, and wonders are not for today, they nevertheless still follow those who believe. In a community of believers, signs of one sort or another occur (Mark 16:17, 18).

One of the nine charismata listed in 1 Corinthians 12 is the working of miracles (v. 10). "The working of miracles is a manifestation of power beyond the ordinary course of natural law. It is a divine enablement to do something that could not be done naturally."[7] As a gift of the Holy Spirit to the church, God distributes it to whomsoever He will and causes it to function at such times as it pleases Him.

"Miracles, signs, and wonders were commonly accepted in the early church; and leaders led the way in giving place to such ministry. Also, the early church leaders prayed for miracles (Acts 4:30), seeing them not as random, occasional events, but as worthy evidences of God's anointing continually glorifying Christ through the church, and therefore to be sought and welcomed."[8]

DISCERNING THE SOURCE OF MIRACLES

Those who serve in leadership must possess the ability to discern between false and true miracles. They in turn must teach others such discernment. We would be in error to discount the reality of the miracles wrought by the magicians in Egypt. They were not mere tricks or sleight of hand. R. C. Trench writes, "The gods of Egypt, the spiritual powers of wickedness which underlay, and were the informing soul of, that dark and evil kingdom, were in conflict with the God of Israel."[9]

The magicians worked real miracles, but the miracles only went so far. The fact that evil spirits can produce miracles is sufficient evidence that miracles cannot be appealed to absolutely and finally in proof of the doctrine that the worker of them proclaims (Deut. 13:1–5). In a day when New Age teaching has become accepted by many, it behooves every Christian leader to be equipped with spiritual discernment.

FAITH ALIVE

How have you benefited by the study of miracles, signs, and wonders in the Old and New Testaments?

What do you understand to be the purposes of miracles, signs, and wonders?

1. *The New Bible Dictionary*, J. D. Douglas, Organizing Ed. (Grand Rapids, MI: Wm. B. Eerdmans Publishing Co., 1962), 828, "Miracles."

2. Ibid., 1185, "Sign, 4. Works of God."

3. James Strong, *The New Strong's Exhaustive Concordance of the Bible; Greek Dictionary of the New Testament* (Nashville, TN: Thomas Nelson Publishers, 1990), #*1411*.

4. Ibid., #*4592*.

5. Ibid., #*5059*.

6. Ibid., #*1140*.

7. *Spirit-Filled Life Bible* (Nashville, TN: Thomas Nelson Publishers, 1991), 1736–1737, note on 1 Cor. 12:8–11.

8. Ibid., 1627, "Kingdom Dynamics: Acts 2:22, Miracles, Signs, and Wonders."

9. R. C. Trench, *Notes on the Miracles of Our Lord* (Grand Rapids, MI: Baker Book House, 1949), 15.

Lesson 12/Acknowledgment of Dreams and Visions

Many books have been written on the subject of traits for spiritual leaders. But few address the value of the supernatural, such as dreams, visions, miracles, signs, wonders, and the gifts of the Spirit. Yet supernatural phenomena have accompanied spiritual leaders from Abraham to the apostles. And there are no scriptures that indicate that these were to be discontinued. Instead, they are presented in the New Testament as legitimate, credible, and desirable assets for spiritual leadership today.

DREAMS

When there was not yet a written revelation, and there was not yet an established order of prophets, God would often give direction to His people through dreams. He spoke through dreams during the time of the patriarchs and the judges. God also spoke through dreams on special occasions.

Though we live in a time when we have a full written revelation, and a time when the Holy Spirit indwells the believer, guidance through dreams may still be given by God.

On dreams and visions Jamie Buckingham comments, "On his missionary journey Paul planned a northward turn into Bithynia. But that night he dreamed of a man begging him, 'Come over to Macedonia and help us' (v. 9). On the basis of the dream, Paul altered his direction, and thus exemplifies a trait of Holy Spirit-guided leaders. While ungodly leaders consult horoscopes and diviners for direction in their lives, godly leaders hear from God 1) through the written Word, the Bible, and 2) through dreams and visions (2:17). Their thought channels are cleansed of impurity (2 Cor. 10:5). They are not conformed to the pattern of this world but are transformed by the renewing of their minds (Rom. 12:2). Their affections are on things above (Col. 3:2).

Therefore, when the Holy Spirit chooses to speak to them through visions (daytime mind pictures) and dreams (sleeping revelations), they hear clearly (see also Ps. 16:7; Acts 9:10; 10:3, 17; 18:9)."[1]

 WORD WEALTH

Dream, *enupnion* (en–*oop*–neon), means a supernatural suggestion or impression received during sleep, a sleep-vision.[2]

The Bible condemns dreams resulting from divination. Divination is the art or practice that seeks to foresee or foretell future events or discover hidden knowledge by the aid of demonic supernatural powers. A diviner is one that practices divination. The Bible forbids consulting persons who practice such arts (Deut. 18:10–12).

An examination of dreams in Scripture reveals that there are two kinds of dreams: 1) Those that are made up of ordinary dream phenomena in which the one who dreams sees a series of images that relate to events in his or her everyday life, such as the butler's dream in Genesis 40:9–13 and the baker's dream in verses 16–19; and 2) dreams that communicate a message from God, as in the cases of Abimelech's dream in Genesis 20:3–7 and Solomon's in 1 Kings 3:5–15.

In Hebrew thought, there was a close connection between dreaming and prophesying (Jer. 23:25, 32). In the days of Samuel and Saul, it was commonly believed that God communicated through dreams as well as through Urim and the prophets (1 Sam. 28:6).

OLD TESTAMENT DREAMS

God revealed His will frequently in Old Testament days in dreams, and there were those who could interpret them. An interesting dream was given to a Philistine king named Abimelech. Genesis 20 tells the story about this dream. Read the chapter and then enter your answers to the following questions.

What motivated Abraham to say Sarah was his sister?

What might possibly have happened had not God intervened with the dream He gave to Abimelech? How would that have affected the promise God had made to Abraham that he would have a son by his wife Sarah? (Gen. 17:15, 16)

What evidence do you find that Abimelech took the dream seriously?

FAITH ALIVE

As you read the story, in what ways do you identify with Abraham? His fear? Not telling the truth? Risking the fulfillment of God's promise in your life because of sin?

Did you find it interesting that the one who had been lied to was prayed for by the one who did the lying, and God answered the latter's prayer? What does that reveal about God's mercy and grace?

Joseph was the son of Jacob and Rachel (Gen. 30:22–24). Jacob had several sons, but he loved Joseph more than the others (37:3). When Joseph was seventeen, his father gave him a "tunic [coat] of many colors" (v. 3). This suggested to the family members that Jacob had chosen Joseph to be their prince and priest. Further, it indicated that he intended to pass the birthright to Joseph. Because of this paternal partiality, Joseph was hated by his brothers (vv. 3, 4). And Joseph's relationship with his brothers was not at all improved when he told them of his dreams of personal exaltation (vv. 7, 9).

He had two unusual prophetic dreams that are recorded in Genesis 37:5–10. After you have read this passage in the Scriptures, respond to the following questions.

Why did Joseph's brothers become angry when he told them his dreams?

How did Joseph's father respond to Joseph's dreams?

Do you think Joseph was cocky as he related his dreams to his brothers? Was he flaunting his "favored son" status?

Do you think Joseph understood the prophetic nature of the dreams? If he did, was he wise in sharing them with his family?

Joseph's dreams of exaltation were fulfilled. Pharaoh gave Joseph his signet ring, which meant that he was given the highest office dealing with financial matters (Gen. 41:42–44).

Joseph and his brothers were reconciled when they came before him in Egypt (45:1–9). They did indeed humbly bow before him (42:6) just as Joseph had seen in his prophetic dream (37:5–8).

The Pharaoh who ruled Egypt at the time of Joseph's imprisonment had two dreams that troubled him greatly (Gen.

41:1–7). None of Pharaoh's scribes or magicians could interpret the dreams for him. The chief butler, whose dream Joseph had interpreted when they both were prisoners, suddenly remembered the promise he had made to help Joseph when he was restored to his position in Pharaoh's court. He told Pharaoh of the prison incident and how Joseph was gifted in interpreting dreams. Joseph was sent for and was brought before Pharaoh. But before interpreting Pharaoh's dreams, Joseph gave God the glory by saying, "It is not in me; God will give Pharaoh an answer of peace" (v. 16). Then he proceeded to interpret the dreams (vv. 25–32). Read the interpretation of the dreams and then answer the following questions.

What did Joseph mean when he said, "The dreams of Pharaoh are one"? (v. 25)

Why was the dream given twice to Pharaoh?

Why do you suppose God chose to work through Joseph in the interpretation of Pharaoh's dreams?

 FAITH ALIVE

Joseph resisted pride when he prefaced the interpretation of Pharaoh's dreams by giving glory to the God who enabled him to do the interpreting. Tell of an occasion in your own life when you were able to give God glory for some way in which He used you in His ministry to help others.

What practical benefit was derived from Joseph's interpretation of Pharaoh's dreams? (vv. 33–36)

 PROBING THE DEPTHS

Just as there were false prophets in the Old Testament who claimed to speak from the premise of a God-given dream, but in fact had not received such a dream, so there have been false prophets in every age since. There are false prophets today who claim to speak for God but in reality seek to lead people away from Him. God says to beware of them, "Beware of false prophets, who come to you in sheep's clothing, but inwardly they are ravenous wolves" (Matt. 7:15).

Read Matthew 7:16–20. Write down the way in which we may detect or identify false prophets .

What is meant by "Therefore by their fruits you will know them"? (v. 20)

There are many more Old Testament scriptures that deal with dreams. Read the following passages in the left column to discover the persons in the dreams, and then record your discoveries. Record in the two right columns the nature of the dream and the outcome of any action that was directed.

	Persons Involved	Nature of Dream	Outcome of Action
Gen. 28:10–16			

	Persons Involved	Nature of Dream	Outcome of Action
1 Kin. 3:5–15			
Job 7:11–16			

NEW TESTAMENT DREAMS OF DIRECTION

As was pointed out earlier, dreams recorded in the Bible are of two kinds: ordinary dream phenomena and dreams which communicate a message from God. As we turn to dreams in the New Testament, we find that Joseph's first dream was a message from God.

JOSEPH

It takes little imagination to appreciate the very human dilemma in which Joseph found himself when he received the devastating news that Mary, his wife-to-be, was already pregnant. Though she had explained the supernatural nature of her pregnancy, Joseph found it hard to believe. He decided to divorce Mary. Unlike our modern engagements, a pledge to marriage in Joseph and Mary's day was legally binding and could be broken only by divorce. Because he was an upright man, Joseph planned to divorce Mary quietly to save embarrassment.

While Joseph thought about these things, an angel of the Lord appeared to him in a dream. Summarize the angel's message to Joseph (Matt. 1:20, 21):

Summarize Joseph's actions in response to the message (Matt. 1:22–25):

FAITH ALIVE

Put yourself in Joseph's place. How would you have felt had you gotten the news that he got regarding Mary's pregnancy?

What would you have considered doing?

Why do you think God spoke to Joseph in a dream?

Name any cases you know of when people received a dream they believed to be from God, obeyed its direction, and experienced its fulfillment.

If you believe God has sent a dream to you, note how these verses can guide your response—1 Thessalonians 5:8, 11–13, 16–22; 1 Corinthians 13.

VISIONS

"The revelation of the word and will of God to man by the inspiration of the Holy Spirit involves besides the dream . . . the phenomenon of supernatural vision. Whereas the dream occurs only during sleep, the vision is more vividly perceived by the physical sense of sight and occurs more normally when one is awake (Gen. 46:2; Num. 24:4, 16; Dan. 10:7; Acts 9:7; 10:9). However, the human agent of the vision, under the overpowering influence of the divine presence, frequently oscillates between the sleeping and the waking state (Zech. 4:1, 2; Lk. 9:32; Rev. 1:17)."³

WORD WEALTH

Vision, *hazon* (hay–*zon*), comes from a Hebrew root word used to describe the beholding of a vision by the seer while in an ecstatic state (Is. 1:1; Ezk. 12:27); while the word *mar'a,* from the ordinary root 'to see,' means vision as a means of revelation (Num. 12:6; 1 Sam. 3:15). The New Testament uses two words in this connection: *horama* (Acts 9:10, 12; 10:3, 17, 19) and *optasia* (Lk. 1:22; Acts 26:19; 2 Cor. 12:1). They signify 'appearance' or 'vision.' The emphasis seems to be upon the ecstatic nature of the experience, and the revelatory character of the knowledge, which came to the biblical prophets and seers. The experience points to a special awareness of God shared by saintly men (e.g. Jer. 1:11; Dan. 2:19; Acts 9:10; 16:9), and to God's readiness to reveal Himself to men (Ps. 89:19; Acts 10:3).⁴

VISIONS AND REVIVALS

Visions that are given as a means of communicating God's word are also associated with revival. Read the following references and note the manner in which this is true.

Ezekiel 12:21–25

Joel 2:28; Acts 2:17

Who are the persons who will dream dreams?

Who will see visions?

In what sense are dreams and visions associated with revival?

WHEN THERE IS NO VISION

Spiritual health wanes when there is no vision. Symptoms of such a condition are: 1) neglect of God's Word; 2) "lip-service" religion; and 3) not giving God first place in one's heart. The following scriptures reveal times in Israel's history when there was no vision. Read the verses and describe the condition.

Condition that Prevailed

Isaiah 29:9–12

Lamentations 2:9

Micah 3:6

Ezekiel 7:26

First Samuel 3:1 describes a time of declension in Israel's history with these words, "Now the boy Samuel ministered to the Lord before Eli. And the word of the Lord was rare in those days; there was no widespread revelation." The *New International Version* of the Bible translates the last half of the same verse in this way, "In those days the word of the Lord was rare; there were not many visions."

NEW TESTAMENT VISIONS

Of the New Testament writers, Luke seems to show the greatest interest in visions. Read the following scriptures and then write the person's name to whom the vision came and the nature of the vision.

	Person Who Received Vision	Nature of Vision
Luke 1:5, 8, 9–22		
Acts 9:10		
Acts 10:3–8		
Acts 10:9–48		
Acts 18:9–11		

CONCLUSION

As one studies the lives of biblical visionaries, it becomes apparent that all were persons of intelligence and action. Visions were not experiences that they sought after, but visions came to some who were seeking that which divine visions bear—the word of the Lord.

It is clear in the New Testament that young men will see visions and old men will dream dreams (Joel 2:28; Acts 2:17). Though we are not told to seek visions and dreams, at the same time we should be open to them and receive them in faith. What we must seek and obey—however God sends it—is His clear and living word.

1. *Spirit-Filled Life Bible* (Nashville, TN: Thomas Nelson Publishers, 1991), 1658, "Kingdom Dynamics: Acts 16:6–10, Dreams and Visions."

2. *The Analytical Greek Lexicon: New Testament* (New York: Harper and Brothers Publishers), 143.

3. "Vision," *Baker's Dictionary of Theology* (Grand Rapids, MI: Baker's Book House, 1960), 545.

4. "Vision," *The New Bible Dictionary*, J.D. Douglas, Ed. (Grand Rapids, MI: Eerdmans Publishing Co., 1962), 1312–1313.

Epilogue

As you have worked your way through this book, you have probably experienced a wide range of reactions. Perhaps one was a greater appreciation for the obedience, or commitment, of godliness, or the humility of those you know who serve in places of spiritual leadership. As you see them confidently minister, encourage faith in their followers, and contend for the Holy Spirit's anointing, you understand more fully God's sovereign call upon their lives.

If your reaction to this study has been one of desire to serve God in spiritual leadership, consult your pastor and other leaders who will be able to direct you about preparing yourself more fully for such service.

Perhaps your reaction was one of despair. You said to yourself, "How could I ever become a spiritual leader? I feel so inadequate." Regardless of your feelings of inadequacy, if God has called you to serve in leadership in His kingdom, He will provide all that you need to become the leader He has called you to be. Jesus said, "Follow Me, and I will make you fishers of men" (Matt. 4:19). It is ours to follow, and His to make us to be what He wants us to be.

Be assured that the One who calls you will be patient, loving, and forgiving as He develops the traits of leadership in you. He is also the One who will empower you to accomplish the things He calls you to do. His grace is sufficient, and He will perfect that which concerns you (see Ps. 138:8; Phil. 1:6; 1 Peter 5:10).